NEW HORIZONS
IN
CREATIVE THINKING:

A Survey and Forecast

RELIGION AND CIVILIZATION SERIES

RELIGION AND CIVILIZATION SERIES

NEW HORIZONS
IN
CREATIVE THINKING:

A Survey and Forecast

EDITED BY

R. M. MacIver

LIEBER PROFESSOR EMERITUS OF POLITICAL PHILOSOPHY
AND SOCIOLOGY, COLUMBIA UNIVERSITY

GREENWOOD PRESS, PUBLISHERS
WESTPORT, CONNECTICUT

Library of Congress Cataloging in Publication Data

Institute for Religious and Social Studies, Jewish
    Theological Seminary of America.
    New horizons in creative thinking.

    (Religion and civilization series)
    Reprint of the ed. published by the Institute for
Religious and Social Studies, New York.
    Includes index.
    CONTENTS: Shapley, H. Human ideals and the cosmic
view.--Boas, G. Philosophy and the art of living.--
Hofstadter, A. The arts and contemporary life. [etc.]
    1. Intellectual life--Addresses, essays, lectures.
2. Creation (Literary, artistic, etc.)--Addresses,
essays, lectures. I. MacIver, Robert Morrison, 1882-
1970. II. Title. III. Series.
CB425.I54   1975   909.82'5   75-26660
ISBN 0-8371-8371-5

41324

Originally published in 1954 by The Institute for Religious
and Social Studies, New York

Reprinted with the permission of Harper & Row, Publishers, Inc.

Reprinted in 1975 by Greenwood Press,
a division of Williamhouse-Regency Inc.

Library of Congress Catalog Card Number 75-26660

ISBN 0-8371-8371-5

Printed in the United States of America

This volume contains the series of luncheon addresses delivered at The Institute for Religious and Social Studies of The Jewish Theological Seminary of America during the winter of 1953–1954. We regret that Mr. Lewis Mumford was unable to prepare for publication the impressive talk he contributed to the program.

Each chapter in this volume represents solely the individual opinion of the author. Neither the Institute nor the editor assumes responsibility for the views expressed. We have been fortunate enough to enlist a group of authors each of whom has distinctive knowledge in his own field, and the Institute is indeed grateful for the generous way in which they have responded to its invitation.

CONTENTS

PREFACE

Since the Institute was first established no set of luncheon addresses has received more attention or aroused more interest than the series now presented to the reader; and there were many requests for advance copies of them. The editor believes that they should appeal equally in their printed form. They are thought-stimulating. Each writer offers a perspective on some aspect of the cultural life of our time, and his assessment of it is in effect his judgment concerning the new demands that our age makes on the creative genius and the social wisdom of our artists and thinkers. Each of our contributors has his own viewpoint. They speak with different voices, and they provoke the reader to think for himself. It is unlikely that any reader could agree with them all, but he can find in them all something well worth pondering over.

We begin with our cosmographer, who brilliantly views our age and our humanity against the moving eternities of time and space. We then have two philosophers who perceptively relate the fine arts to that other difficult art, the art of living. Then we have a number of authorities each of whom takes a particular area of our creative culture—the novel, poetry, and literature in general, and music and painting and the drama and television—and looks through the present to the signs of the times ahead. Here the reader will be challenged by certain differences of emphasis and outlook shown by our various contributors. Henry D. Cowell wholeheartedly aligns himself with the new directions in music and foresees future developments stemming out of them. But in the fields of literature our authors in various degrees reflect on the shortcomings of the present style. Melville Cane feels that in poetry "the great gift of song" is muted because of intellectual or technical preoccupations. William G. Rogers senses the need for literature that "cuts back underneath our glittering plastic surfaces and reaches flesh and bone." Oscar J.

Campbell is genuinely pessimistic about the spiritual quality of our literary output.

In a somewhat similar vein Ben Shahn, after reviewing the rise of non-objective art, believes that the new horizons "lie across despondent swamps and difficult hills that might dampen the courage even of the dauntless Christian of *The Pilgrim's Progress*." And Walter Kerr is convinced that the theater has gone astray because instead of minding its proper business it has heeded the siren voices of sociology and politics. On the other hand, Robert Saudek envisages great potential contributions of television to the intellectual and cultural life of our time.

Back of these views lies the question of the relation between art and morals and of the effects of the infusion of particular moral objectives into the work of the artist. Two approaches to this question are offered respectively by W. G. Constable and John Ferren. Finally we enter, under the guidance of Harold D. Lasswell, into the new developing area of the art that ministers to the understanding and the improvement of human relations, in the factory, in the camp, and in the give-and-take of everyday life.

So we range from the astronomical observatory to the studio and from the ivory tower to the industrial plant. Everywhere there is movement and the breath of change. Everywhere today is merging into tomorrow, with its old problems and its new hopes.

THE EDITOR

NEW HORIZONS IN CREATIVE THINKING:

A Survey and Forecast

I

HUMAN IDEALS AND THE COSMIC VIEW

BY

HARLOW SHAPLEY

My assignment to address an assembly of clergymen on the ideals needed for New Horizons leads me to inquire: What is wrong with the old horizons? Certainly they are not worn out. In these days of routine living we rarely budget time for contemplating goals, to say nothing of reaching for them. Not much attention is paid to the distant lights that glimmer and beckon toward new horizons. The customary patterns and popular parroting suit us pretty well—most of us. We are resigned to what is, and the grooves of the pattern and the bromides of the parrot are comfortable. Emphasis on the near and the immediate tempers our worry of what lies far ahead in time and far away in space. Moreover, the horizons, when we do timidly look at them, appear to be infected with nightmares and inhabited by misanthropic dragons. We relish neither.

Perhaps we need not so much a shiny new set of horizons as a revised model—we want broader fenders, faster pick-up, better vision, higher respect for the rules of the road, greater trust in what lies over the hill, and a feeling for the worth of our itinerary.

The horizons of the past decade or two doubtless could now be profitably readjusted. Adjusted with profit, that is, if we who seek them for ourselves and for others would bring the evaluations of goals into keeping with our understanding of man and the universe.

If I sound grim and solemn thus far, I regret the gloom; but the Destiny of Man is not a lightsome topic.

In the world of protoplasmic organisms man is an extraordinary construct. He is forever looking over his shoulder backwards, and sometimes timidly far forward. He is unique in this respect. The tree and flower do not bother about the planning of new horizons. The beast and the bug likewise have presently no goals that differ from those of the Pliocene. They live a routine pattern; their programs are clear. Individual survival through self-defense, physical continuity and growth through the ingestion of familiar and habitual foods, propagation of offspring in the interest of survival of the family and species— these are the facts and acts in the life-struggle of the bees and flowers.

But man, while sharing with other organisms the vital drives and goals, has got himself into a transcendency where survival is not necessarily a major inspiration. He seeks goals that involve more than his own fate. The enlarged frontal lobes of his brain have brought with them the concepts and the performance of charity, altruism, and mutual respect; and also greed, mendacity, distrust, and similar less happy qualities. These are human qualities, or at least they are more strongly manifest in man than in the less thoughtful and less scheming animals.

This mental complex, this forebrain of the most specialized primate, has so complicated his life that programs for living now appear essential. And the program-planning requires a philosophy of living and of life which we describe as an assembly of ideals. So defined, we can probably say with reason that ideals, programs of life, are indulged in deliberately by man but not by plants and the other animals. I do not feel too sure about this argument. Are we not rather hasty in asserting that the varied artifacts and ceremonies of animals, such as those of the social insects, are purely instinctive, no matter how complex and how peculiarly adapted they are to conditions of the moment? And are we not equally hasty in saying that men are thought-guided animals in spite of the evidence that mostly we react rather than think?

The acceptance of the dogma that we, the higher *hominidae,* are superior beings—an assumption based on our religious creeds and preliminary scientific analyses—strikes me as an indication of incompetent cosmic outlook. The superior-race dogma of Central Europe two decades ago was shattered by war and by anthropological research; but even so it is doggedly retained by colonial governments the world over. Now we are also confronted with the superior-species presumption.

Let us look further into the hypothesis that we alone make programs for living and work toward ethereal ideals. We shall not question the present physical dominance of man over other animals on a small planet in a run-of-the-mill solar system near the rim of a routine but oversize galaxy. There are more than two billions of men, but all are included in one species. Notwithstanding some variety in color, stature, and clothing habits, man and the proverbial pea-in-the-pod follow a monotonous standard. The *Homo* has two arms and two legs and one nose. Quite foolish of me to emit such an obviosity? No. If some men had three legs or four arms or as many smellers as a butterfly, we could easily and reasonably fabricate a superior-inferior-race hypothesis. The wasps, for instance, do have such a diversity; there are hundreds of species, and by one criterion or another we might easily sort out "superior" races, which doubtless would have remoter horizons than their inferiors possess and would have different "ideals" in their labor of horizon-seeking.

The ecological horizons of the insects change slowly with the geological ages. Some minor adjustments they make promptly, however, as a result of man's economic interference. For example, his intercontinent commerce has brought to North America the Dutch elm disease and the Japanese beetle. These organisms, at their own level, now have some new or at least expanded horizons. And, similarly, through his commerce and cultural growth man has greatly disturbed his own old environments, both material and spiritual. In consequence his physical and psychical horizons and programs are changing.

Now I see that I can answer my opening question: What is wrong with the old horizons? Nothing much. They were good in their day and for their clientele. The need for new horizons arises simply because the terrain has changed. The old horizons no longer fit. What were sometimes steep uphill climbs are now gentle downhill ski runs. What had appeared, to our insufficiently trained minds, to be conquered and occupied territory has bristled up with doubts and mysteries and perhaps impossible barriers. The ingenuity of the rather ingenuous primate has re-ordered the terrain, set up new values, and brought to him a questioning confusion.

Let us look toward some of these altered horizons and see if yesterday's ideals may still suffice. And on the way let us wonder if we can assuredly maintain ourselves above the animal level. The ants, bees, termites, and wasps are social groups of great antiquity that have developed many morphological specialties and social characteristics. Forty million years before man appeared they had successful social relations in a variety of forms. Then, as now, they practised the higher virtues and some of the most intricate technologies. Altruism, cooperation among individuals, and patriotism are natural to scores of different kinds of the hymenopterous insects. Some of them know and use community sanitation, air conditioning, anesthesia, birth control, fungus culture, and of course the making of wax, honey, and paper. They have long displayed numerous talents to which man has only presently attained.

These astonishing well-tried social developments, which came about long before nature devised the higher primates out of a humbler past, should be kept in mind when we later contemplate the heights to which biological evolution may have gone on the livable planets scattered throughout the cosmos. And we must be ready to believe that high developments can elsewhere occur. They probably parallel the biological adventures on this planet's surface, for we find the same cosmic chemistry in distant galaxies as in our own, the same responses to gravitation, the same relationships between matter, energy, space, and time. The nature of physics and chemistry is apparently the same everywhere. Therefore we expect to find, wherever our telescopes lead us, the same sort of organic chemical reactions, when the physical conditions permit the existence of organisms. Whatever life exists elsewhere necessarily should be similar to the life here—similar even if not identical, similar in pattern and quality. But elsewhere there may have been more time for some phases of biological evolution, or better topographic environments, or more propitious characteristics of stellar radiation or planetary stability, to the end that the high life could go higher, perhaps much higher, than anything we know.

Returning to terrestrial man, we note that he seems to be in a biological groove with little prospect of early escape from the rut of physical uniformity. Is there more hope for freedom mentally than biologically? We seem to think in grooves. But spiritually we can individually be explorers—uncramped by grooves and barriers. Can be, but are we?

On this planet we now are, as remarked above, dominant and dominating among fellow creatures. We are rich in numbers, though of course relatively scarce when compared with bacteria, or with insects and some species of fish. We are dominant in power over other life; but there is nothing to strut about in this situation. We are dominant only in this current Psychozoic Era, as the giant lizards were dominant in the Mesozoic Era a hundred million years ago, the cockroaches in the preceding Paleozoic Era, and the trilobites two hundred million years earlier.

These comparisons, however, orient mankind only with respect to the life forms on this one planet. We should broaden our views concerning life by forsaking for a few moments this earth and its thin superficial infection of protoplasm. We can then search for biological developments beyond the atmosphere. Acting as your agent in cosmic computation and analysis, I find the probabilities are extremely high that there is life elsewhere. I say that too dogmatically, but it is with the same assurance that I say, without visual checking, that there are mountains on the unobserved back side of the moon, that iron is in the center of the earth, that hydrogen atoms are wandering in intergalactic space, and that there is snow on the mountains of Tibet that I have never seen. Deduction is sometimes quite as convincing and reliable as ocular recording.

In surveying your new horizons, and in formulating your programmatic ideals, you would do well to keep always in mind that this universe includes a great many experiments in the higher biologies. Doubtless numerous domiciles of life have produced beings more sentient than we, beings more comprehending, more experiencing, and possibly, by their unimaginable standards, more divine than we. (You are of course at liberty to deny, as categorically as I affirm, the existence of these other-world carriers of "spirit"; but why not face the evidence and think it through?)

Recently I published the simple reckoning on which I base the foregoing statement that life of the higher sort, which here we associate with man, birds, insects, and other animals, is not a local terrestrial affair only. And I repeat—for it is important in horizon adjustments —I repeat that life has probably produced elsewhere forms that excel anything that this planet can show. It is not difficult to see how improvements could be made, however you define "improvements." For example, man has not enough well-developed sense organs to tell him what is going on. We have no good physiological register of electric waves and must resort to gadgetary feelers. We have no bodily organ for sensing directly the ultraviolet, or the infrared. Some stars have enormous magnetic fields; ours has a relatively weak one. We have no recognizable magnetic sense organ; it may naturally be otherwise elsewhere. (Some birds appear to be usefully equipped with a good magnetic sense, if not a magnetic sense organ.)

As every anatomist knows, man is physically primitive in many respects, and in others rather dangerously specialized. His primitivism and his physiological oddities (brains, for example) may erase him suicidally from the earth. His clinging to the past keeps him most of the time at the animal level—food, fight, shelter, procreation. His reaching for heaven and the stars may disconnect him from his animal sources of physical and neurological strength.

Apparently up to this point I am not very optimistic about *Homo.* But my doubts refer to the past and the present. What lies ahead is another judgment. With new horizons recognized, and ideals continually adjusted to the growth of man's knowledge, the man of the future can perhaps justify our inclination to glorify him as the central showpiece in a new biological kingdom.

Postponing a further interview with the stars, and I am sure they have plenty of time, let us look around, far, wide, and back a billion years in earth history. We recognize in the animal world two kingdoms—animal and vegetable. Are they the only organic kingdoms that can be produced on this planet? On remote and happier planets there may be life forms other than plant and animal—other major kingdoms of life.

But have we not right here on earth the beginning of a third major category—the Psychozoic Kingdom? Now I know it is vanity, almost anthropocentrism, to sort out *Homo sapiens* and say that he differs so much from the chimpanzees, spiders, and oysters that he merits a kingdom of his own—differs so much that we can set up for him a separate set of natural laws, much as we can separate the rules for plants from the rules for animals. But vanity and hopeful wishing aside, the evidence is good that the forebrain—our large time-binding cortex—makes a great difference in the animate world, and perhaps justifies the separate classification.

We cannot draw a sharp boundary between man and fellow animal. Certainly we developed from simpler, less thoughtful organic forms. The series is continuous from lowest algae to highest primates. Perhaps the chimps, the termites, and the orchids will not object, if we are properly modest about it, and claim only that we believe we are now on the way to the establishment of a Psychozoic Kingdom, where brain overshadows brawn, rationality overshadows natural instinct.

I have almost brought myself to the point of believing that man is important in the universe. But I want you to keep in mind that this psychozoic development, now blossoming among the higher primates on this planet, has probably long since been fully attained in other inhabited worlds. At this point in our contemplations we begin to glimpse a cosmic goal for ourselves. Although we are out of touch (except in the imagination) with the high-life organisms elsewhere, we can compete with them, as the eras roll along, in advancing the *third biological kingdom*. We see faintly a mystical light aglimmer on a new horizon.

As the free-moving animals outdo the anchored sunshine-sucking plants from which they sprang, so do we free-thinking humans outdo our ancestral animals, anchored to their instincts. To advance further toward ultimate goals, it is clear that our emphasis in a program-for-life should turn away more and more from the animal—turn, shall I say, toward the angelic. If you are allergic to angels, turn then toward the spiritual—spiritual, broadly spoken.

I have hinted at new horizons at the cosmic level. On the local terrestrial plane there are also obvious reasons to readjust the horizons. Not exhausting the list, I name three examples.

First, in compliance with the principle and command to love our fellow men, we have long done lipservice, but practically we have not always liked the idea. Fellow man is often repugnant. We keep away from most of him most of the time—we send small gifts. But the world has shrunk. In spite of political and other barriers, we are now all neighbors. The interest in, and love and respect for off-color fellows of the human race is changed in character from that of a century ago. Such a *pandemic philanthropism* is one of the new human horizons.

And here is another which comes to us from the new cosmography. The plaguy astronomers have probed so deep and so far that we can no longer accept, without great uneasiness, the comfortable ideas about time and space of a few decades ago. We have been deposed by the scientists from physical importance in the universe, and made ephemeral and peripheral. No longer is there much cosmic esteem for a vain and strutting man-animal. It is a hard pill to swallow, this cosmic humility; but we no longer doubt the facts. Our God, or gods, as the case may be, or Deity, or First Cause, have much more on His, their, its "hands" than a paternal concern for peripheral, transient, terrestrial primates—much more on hand than a kindly care for the biota of one planet.

The Universe, it seems to me (who am, by the way, a religious man —on my definition of religion), is much more glorious than the prophets of old reported; and we are actors in a greater show than the old billing led us to expect. Knowing what I now know, I would blush to be caught redhanded with the world concepts of two millennia ago. A *proper cosmic orientation* is this second horizon, new to most of us.

Third, the human mind was considered fairly private until recently, largely because we did not know enough about it to justify an exhibition in the marketplace. But now the senses have been dissected, the electric currents of the nerves have been measured, brain waves have become diagnostic, and much of our inner life that we thought was beyond reach of measuring instruments and analyzers is out in plain sight on the drawingboards. Here we find another horizon that needs adjusting; both for those who talk and think of matters spiritual, and for those who indulge themselves (and serve the rest of us) in the realm of the cultural arts. We must be more *mindful of the mind*.

Thus in these three sample realms—worldwide social relations, the physical universe, and the human mind—new opportunities arise for adjustment of our horizons.

Is there anything useful I can say about ideals for the new horizons? Not much that would be helpful because the task of ideal-construction, it seems to me, is best accomplished by the individual who knows his own hidden abilities and limitations, and knows best how to fit life's programs onto his life's past. But I have a few general remarks.

The ideals that spiritual leaders advocate are, in my opinion, of high importance—more important, in the long run, than the political ideals of our puzzled diplomats. In our biological program of establishing the Psychozoic Kingdom, the non-material grows in significance. The clergy are among the keepers of the non-material. *Openmindedness with respect to the growth and bearing of knowledge of the material world* is a high-priority requirement for the set of adjusted ideals. To me the *Discorso,* two years ago, of Pope Pius XII, at the opening of a meeting of the Vatican Academy of Sciences, was epochal. He surveyed and accepted the approximate truth of the recent advances in nuclear physics and in cosmogony. He outlined clearly the nature of atomic energy and of atomic fission, and presented the evidence that the beginning of the world, as we see it, was a few thousand million years ago. It was a notable statement from a notable leader of hundreds of millions of his fellow men.

Openmindedness to the progress and proceeds of the human intellect—that is, for you, if you will accept it, the first ideal. Reoriented piety is second, and follows naturally.

II

PHILOSOPHY AND THE ART OF LIVING

BY

GEORGE BOAS

Probably the most difficult problem which confronts the philosopher is the conflict between time and eternity, the many and the one, the changing and the immutable. We live in time, surrounded by multiple and changing objects, seeking to unify, even to immobilize if possible, the flow of events. We live with individuals, we strive to incorporate them into classes. We see separate and diverse things, we strive to organize them into homogeneous groups. Thus we speak of humanity and come into contact with human beings, different, peculiar, deviating from the scientific norm, recalcitrant to unification. We speak of dogs, cats, and horses, and yet never see or speak to anything other than particular specimens of these classes whose differences from the generalized descriptions found in the books are so great as to lead us to distrust all science. We read about tragedies, comedies, landscapes, and portraits, sonatas, fugues, and symphonies, but we read *Hamlet* and *The Merry Wives of Windsor,* the particular work of art, not the class. We actually listen to the *Appassionata,* not the general class, *sonatas.* We look at Holbein's portrait of Anne of Cleves, not at portraiture. This would appear to be obvious to everyone except philosophers: for they, on the contrary, sometimes maintain that what we see in the specific is the general and indeed unless a work of art somehow or other exemplifies the traits of the general class to which it is supposed to belong, they will have none of it.

At the bottom of all this is the curious feeling that the traits of the class are not only standards by means of which we can tell whether something belongs to that class or not, but are also standards by means of which we can tell whether we should admire it or not. One can understand that a biologist, for instance, would be happier to find in his laboratory a rat or a rabbit which perfectly exemplified the general traits of rat-hood or rabbit-hood than one which was a deviant. If, to be sure, the latter were sufficiently deviant, the biologist would declare that he was not really a rat or a rabbit at all, but some peculiar variety of those animals. But even if we have reason to believe that a tragedy is really the kind of thing described in Aristotle's *Poetics,* why should we prefer tragedies which exemplify that description rather than others? We might reasonably conclude that *Macbeth* differs from *Antigone* in a number of ways, but would it be reasonable to conclude that for that reason it is bad or blameworthy? What obligation has a writer to obey Aristotle or anyone else? I am not maintaining that *Macbeth* is greater than or smaller than Sophocles's *Antigone.* I am simply asking whether (1) if *Antigone* exemplifies the Aristotelian rules, and (2) if *Macbeth* does not, is this evidence for anything more than that the two plays are different? One must of course admit that if an added premise is inserted to the effect that only plays which are Aristotelian are tragedies, then one can conclude that *Macbeth* is not a tragedy. But to conclude that it ought to be a tragedy demands a further premise.

Now all this talk about esthetic criticism is relevant to our topic because even in ethical matters we judge, and probably have to judge, the particular by the general rule. We presumably demand certain abstract principles such as that motive is more important than effect or that the end justifies the means or that one should never break a law. If we find a man doing something of which we disapprove, we condemn him, and presumably can only condemn him, on general grounds. We may say that consequences of his acts were not very harmful but his motives were disgusting, or that his noble motives justified his calamitous behavior. Similarly in esthetic criticism we are likely to say that Bach's fugue in C-major (*Well-tempered Clavier,* Volume I) is a perfect fugue or that *On First Looking into Chapman's Homer* is a perfect sonnet or that the temple to Victory on the Acropolis is a perfect Ionic temple, the perfection consisting in a close approximation to the rules defining each variety or species of works of art. Similarly we might say that the latest Miss America is a perfect physical specimen or that the skeleton of a whale which used to be in the American Museum of Natural History is a perfect whale's skeleton. And if the question is raised of why it is important to be perfect in this sense of the word, the answer, if my own experience counts for anything, is no more than an assumption that the particular should conform to the general rule. That could not be denied if we were convinced that the purpose of artists is conformity, but if we are not so convinced, what is there in this dogma to change our minds?

But suppose we go a step further and declare roundly that such principles are good enough for praising and blaming, but that we are not interested in that activity. We may legitimately wish simply to understand what is before us. We may want to know not merely that Keats's sonnet has fourteen lines and a certain rhyme-scheme but also why its metaphors are based on passive discovery, planets whose position is not calculated in advance but which swim into people's ken, and oceans whose discovery depends not on a previous study of geography but upon accident, and why, moreover, the poet found his basic images in feudalism. To note these things may not give us a greater admiration for the sonnet, but it does give us greater understanding of it. Such a study will not make the piece seem more like other sonnets, but different from them. It will bring out the peculiarities of the poem, not its conformities to other poems or poetic standards. But obviously we shall then find ourselves engaged in arguments with those people who believe the task of the critic to be what they call "evaluation."

We find an analogous situation in the courts of law. There we are not engaged in rewarding but in punishing people. But we have similarly to discover whether the accused actually did or did not perform a certain act which has been given a certain class-name in the statute books. The application of the general principles here to the particular event is so delicate a matter that we find our names of crimes to have changed their meaning often very seriously in the course of time. It would seem an easy matter to define an act so that courts would never have any difficulty in determining whether the act in question was or was not performed. Yet even such apparently simple words as "person," "inherently dangerous instrument," "due process of law," "conspiracy," "knowingly," turn out to be puzzles when one tries to apply them to actual events. In my days of military service, "desertion" was so defined as to include the intention of not returning to one's post. But since such intentions were next to impossible to ascertain, a rough and ready rule had to be devised whereby if a soldier had been absent without leave for ten days, other things being equal, he was supposed to be guilty of desertion and not merely of absence without leave. These rough and ready rules are the most interesting things we have in such situations, for they are an admission of failure on the part of those who believe in the possibility of finding the one in the many, the eternal in the temporal. We find their analogues in science when the scientist excuses his failure to achieve perfection by resorting to the qualifying phrase, "under laboratory conditions." We find them in the practise of admitting extenuating circumstances in ethics or the law. And we find them in esthetic criticism when we admit that matter always deforms the perfection of the rule.

If then we are going to criticize living, we are going to have general rules and we are also going to find that the general rules are followed only by those who deliberately attempt to follow them. For in all these fields there have been men and women who in the first place know next to nothing about the rules and second care very little for obeying those which they do know about. The first group are children and other innocents who grow up under the pressure of societies big and little, families, friends, business groups, gangs, churches, schools, clubs, which already enforce certain codes whose origin they have forgotten, if they ever knew them. One might just as well ask the average undergraduate why he has to go to college for four years instead of three or five to get a bachelor's degree as to ask a child why he must obey his parents or not eat with his fingers. "That is not done," is the ultimate precept, though it reads like a simple description rather than a command. That it is uttered at the precise moment when the thing which is not done is being done, is usually not pointed out by the accused. He is too terrified at the thought of violating a sacred code to be saucy. But the phrase is in itself of interest, for it looks like an attempt to absorb precepts into scientific law. When a physicist says that an acid ought to turn a piece of blue litmus paper red, he means that it always does, under laboratory conditions. But when a teacher says that one ought to tell the truth on all occasions, he means that it would be nice if everyone did tell the truth but they do not. The only similarity between what might be called the scientific or descriptive "ought" and the evaluative or prescriptive "ought" is that both signify an obedience to some general rule. But in the former case what ought to be is, and in the latter it is not. Whether all this boils down to a fact of social psychology, that groups desire conformity rather than rebellion, I have no way of knowing. But looking at the way in which both individuals and groups develop habits and traditions which inevitably take on a compulsive force, the conclusion seems proper.

In fact, we see in all human activities, in language, in customs, in laws, in practical activities such as the various crafts, in all the arts, even in scientific method, a principle of ritualization, analogous to the formation of habits in the life of an individual. It is this which makes it possible for certain historians and sociologists to speak of national traits, of the French spirit, the Greek way of life, the British temper. That we all tend toward ritualization is no excuse for not correcting the tendency, but, on the other hand, if it is a general trait of mankind, then it might be concluded that there is no more escaping it than there is of escaping the desire for food. But even if that is true, there is always the possibility of substituting one rule of life for another, unless forces of which we can never be aware are the controlling factors in our choices. This is no place to develop an argument either for or against free will, but it might be pointed out that if human beings contribute nothing whatsoever to the events in which they participate, they are the only things in the universe, of which we have any knowledge, which are in that position.

It would seem to be precisely in the field of such choices that living becomes an art. For the arts are above all distinguished from other human activities by the element of conscious control. The difference between, for instance, gobbling everything edible which lies before us and growing, storing, and cooking food, is the entrance of reason into the desire to satisfy hunger. There are, I am told, in Australia people who simply gather their food as chickens do, looking under logs for fat grubs, upon stones for lizards, in the moss and green shoots for vegetable matter. The only artistry involved in this behavior would appear to be that involved in the knowledge of what is edible and what is not edible. But the moment an individual or group begins to plant seeds and gather fruit, to domesticate animals for food, and to cook, we quite properly call their activity artistry. The same is true of the satisfaction of all of our desires. It is the difference between the man who slugs his opponent blindly with his fists, feet, stones, and bits of wood, and him who has learned the rudiments of boxing or spear-throwing, or even stone-hurling. There is no mystery about how this is done. We simply learn by experience. But what we learn is that various situations have a kind of similarity and that what has succeeded in an early member of the series will probably succeed also in the later. We thus develop, whether we know it or not, a set of rules. The compulsion of habit is enough to enforce these rules. It is so effective indeed that even when the rules no longer succeed in attaining the end for which they were presumably devised, we will continue to follow them. They will become ceremonious and acquire the sanctity of religious rites. The practises will cease to be practical and will become self-justified. Critics will no longer praise them for their efficacy but for their formal perfection. Thus an art like fencing is no longer practised for self-defense. It is practised as a fine art. No one paints animals any longer, as far as I know, with the idea of obtaining a magical power over them, but with the idea of simply looking at them. In fact, some estheticians would maintain that if an art did have any practical value it would sink from the level of fine art to the level of handicraft. What has happened is the preservation of a manner of doing things, as in social etiquette, ceremonious speech, and, one might add, liberal education.

The evolution of instruments into objects of art is one of the most noticeable and yet unnoticed of human peculiarities. We do not reject obsolete instruments; we preserve them in museums. One can think of no tools which have not become *objets d'art* as soon as they have become useless or at least unused. Architecture is full of such things and even the history of musical forms shows the same development. The art of living as distinguished from unqualified living is the application of what we have learned to the attainment of what we want. We expect the future to repeat the past and when it does we can operate automatically through habit. In such situations consciousness is superfluous. We are in the condition of a pianist who has learned a composition by heart, can sit down at the piano with his eyes blind-folded, and play his piece. He requires no consciousness of what notes he is playing, of the delicate and very complicated motor adjustments which are needed to play anything whatsoever, and in fact would probably be totally unable to tell a questioner how he performs the piece in question. Few of us when speaking are ever conscious of the rules of grammar; we have absorbed them so completely into our system that we need have no awareness of them. We save thought in this way in the literal sense of the phrase. In a highly ritualized society the future would repeat the past. The environment would never change and no new problems would ever arise to demand the use of thinking. We should all act like members of the court of Spain or Austria. We should never know why we act as we do but should all know exactly how to act. Life would become a sort of elaborate dance with a clear and unmistakable pattern. Good manners would be at a premium and the ends of behavior would never be questioned. But this is just what fine art is, according to many estheticians. Fine art, they would have us believe, is a completely ritualized pattern, formal, and self-substantiated. Its works have maximum unity and coherence. In Oscar Wilde's famous phrase, they are utterly useless. And their lack of utility is what makes them fine.

One observes the same sort of thing in universities where something called pure science is valued more highly than applied science. Math-ematics is the purest of all because it need not be put to any practical purpose in order to be justified. Knowledge is valued, as it is said, for its own sake, much as virtue is sometimes said to be its own reward, and beauty, according to Emerson, its own excuse for being. I am far from saying that a mathematician should think about the practical applications of polydimensional geometry before studying it or that an organic chemist should keep his eye on therapeutics while con-ducting his experiments: for we all know that as a matter of fact studies apparently the most remote from practicality have turned out to be the most useful. But one is not forced to engage in a study for its practical value in order to admit that sound theory has practical applications. The most beneficent scientists have often been least concerned with the welfare of society. In fact, it is only a verbal paradox to maintain that a student should above all keep his eye on the truth, not on utility, if he wishes his results to be most useful. The question before us concerns the value of the two sorts of practise and I am merely pointing out the commonplace, that we tend to value pure science higher than applied, fine art higher than crafts, though the latter are, as far as we know, the source of the former. So in the case of language, poetic diction was supposed to be archaic or at least obsolescent diction. Formalized speech became more noble than direct and spontaneous speech. What you could say in conversation you could not write.

The philosopher can do little more about this than to note the facts and the problems which they raise. It would seem clear that if living is to be made an art, there will be both a tendency to ritualization and a tendency toward non-conformity, for the history of all the arts shows innovation as much as tradition. The novel, nature-poetry, the detective story are all innovations in literature. The landscape without figures is an innovation in painting. Abstract and non-objective painting and sculpture are innovations in the plastic arts. But within a narrower field the narrative methods of Defoe, Richardson, Fielding, Jane Austen, Dickens, Henry James, and Joyce show steady change, as well as the retention of something of the past. The same would be true of French painting from David to Matisse. As each innovation is made, it is bound to meet opposition, as well as support, for we have no statistics on the relative numbers of traditionalists and reformers. Tradition gives us a sense of stability and continuity, innovation a sense of discovery and adaptation to new problems.

The art of living, like any other art, begins with the desire to solve problems. We first start to solve any problem whatsoever by seeing whether we do not already possess the answer. It might be reasonably argued that each problem as it arises is new and that therefore we never do have its answer until it is solved. But human beings have a way of maintaining that certain problems are not real, are superficial, trivial, or fantastic. Our tolerance for exceptions is sometimes very great. Consequently the first step in artistry is the acceptance of the problem as real. The next step would probably be that of attempting to solve it in terms of knowledge already acquired, that is, through tradition or custom. If that does not work, then one can either resign oneself to mystery or set up a new hypothesis to cover the matter. All this is platitude, known to anyone who has ever read or even thought about the situation. There is nothing novel in it except possibly the belief which lies behind it, that all artistry is alike in these respects. The painter, the sculptor, the musician always has the choice of accepting the problems of his predecessors, stating them and solving them in their terms, or of perceiving new problems as real and solving them in new terms. There are always artists who belong to schools and movements and even those who do not are likely to find themselves at the head of a new school or movement. It would be folly to deprecate this, for there must be some profound satisfaction in the sense of belonging to a group and of not being always on the periphery of a group. But similarly there must be a drive on the part of the Beethovens and the Prousts to see things in their own way, to investigate the underbrush, to ask *Why,* to say *No.*

To make living into an art then might take two directions, either to ritualize it or to liberate it from all ritual. But neither direction would be fruitful, for ritual will not solve new problems and liberation from all ritual is insanity. There are certain problems which repeat themselves and get solved once and for all. As the environment, including the social environment, changes, the problems obviously change, but sometimes the rate of change is very slow, so slow that it can be neglected. Just where to follow tradition and where to rebel against it are the two basic problems in the art of living and I doubt whether any general rule could be given for answering them. If there were such a rule, ritualization would have taken complete control of life. Living would be analogous to the poetry of the late eighteenth century where every poet seemed to imitate Pope. One can say only that human beings are diverse and that some require more stability in customs than others. The important point is to permit the recalcitrant members of society to be recalcitrant and the traditionalists to be traditionalist. This would not be important in a highly homogeneous society, but certainly it is futile to expect a modern urban society to be all of a piece. The division of labor is such as to give diverse and often conflicting interests to the individuals who compose it. The store of knowledge possessed by the individuals on the basis of which they might be expected to guide their lives is equally diverse. The education which they have received as children is similarly diverse. But diversity is not necessarily bad. Sometimes, to be sure, members of different groups insist that they must exterminate all other groups. They are engaged on a foolish errand, as history shows only too well. One can only suppose that heresies are attempts to satisfy deeply rooted drives. One such drive is what might be called independence of spirit or, if one wants a bad name, pride. Until our generation suppression of heresy always proved impossible. Even today it is wiser to admit the diversity of men's legitimate interests.

This will land one eventually in nominalism, temporalism, pluralism, and even more horrible, relativism. The fact that such names are pejorative may be evidence that the vast majority of philosophers still believe in logical realism, eternalism, monism, and absolutism. We do not know why this is so, as such an attitude raises as many difficulties as its opposite. But one may guess that we have become seduced by the magic of giving a single name to a variety of individuals. If a dozen things have the same name, they must, it seems to be argued, have a common essence. Similarity must, one would think, be explicable only through the presence in diversity of unity. But unity may be simply the unity of origin. One would not *explain,* in any intelligible sense of that word, the Mississippi River by its source. Unity may also be the unity of material. But again if one has five objects made of wood, it is not necessarily the wood which is more interesting than the uses to which the objects are put, the structure of the objects, the cost of the objects, the duration of the objects, or any other characteristic of them. Unity may also be the unity of goal or purpose, sometimes not even achieved when one is studying things. A machine may be made of a variety of substances and yet be designed for a single use. The use is certainly not present in the parts in any literal sense. In fact, the more one examines the argument for essences inherent in a variety of things which have a common name, the more clear it seems that it is based upon a metaphor of substance—just as wood may be present in all wooden objects, so redness or squareness or beauty or goodness may be present. But surely such a usage is permeated with difficulties, as the history of logical realism demonstrates.

One would do better, it would seem, to forget this technique of explanation, that is, the search for a common essence in classes of things and events, and frankly admit that classifications are made for purposes of intellectual organization. In that case the arts as a whole are differentiated from the non-arts as reason is differentiated from what used to be called instinct or perhaps nature. In other words, I am attempting to say that the fundamental distinction is not that between the artistic and the inartistic, but between the artificial and the natural, though both of these adjectives have become so charged with vagueness and ambiguity that it is doubtful whether the substitution does much good. The evidence, however, that a practise is artificial and not natural, as I use these terms, is variation in the former and the lack of it in the latter. Thus our natural functions, such as the circulation of the blood, excretion, digestion, procreation, and so on, go on in the same way in all human beings. But the artificial practises, building houses, speaking, governing, teaching, worshipping, go on in different ways. The differences are to be observed not only from tribe to tribe, but also from epoch to epoch, and sometimes from person to person. What is style in the long run but the individual's peculiar manner of doing certain things? Why does language have a history except that a given people at one time speak differently from the way they speak at other times? If all of us spoke the same language all over the world, and at all periods of human history, no one would think of speech as different from barking or mooing or twittering. Similarly if human beings all built the same kind of shelter, architecture would never have been thought of; our houses would have been classified with spider webs or bird nests.

Living as an art, then, would seem to be predicated on the differences between people rather than on their similarities. We may be all alike in that we have desires which we attempt to satisfy through the arts, but we do not satisfy them in the same way. It is the differences which raise the problems of artistry, not the similarities. I realize that such an emphasis seems to be an accentuation of disorder, indeed of anarchy, and both of those words are bad words. But the fact remains that though we as critics of the human race may deprecate disorder, meaning nothing more than diversity, we have to accept its existence. If we can explain it, we can perhaps justify it.

There are at least the following reasons to believe that diversity in artistry, whether the artistry which eventuates in the usual arts or in the art of living, is inevitable. First, people as individuals have fundamentally different needs. This may be attributable to their so-called original natures, the diversity of their physical structure or not. But that, even in what look to us as simple cultures, some people are better adapted for fighting or hunting or agriculture or fishing than others, should surely need no proof. That the more poorly equipped may be subjected to humiliation and attempt to rival their superiors, also requires no proof. Second, people are born of different parents who are already pretty well oriented in the direction of what they believe to be right and wrong. These parents obviously belong to different economic groups, not merely in that they have different amounts of wealth, but that some are farmers, some small business men, some industrialists, some skilled or unskilled laborers, and so on. They also either belong to some well defined religious group or are irreligious or simply non-religious. They have varying degrees of schooling. Such parents have almost complete power over their children until they send them to school. Thus they fix at a very early and, as we have learned, impressionable, age a set of values in their minds. The children may or may not retain these values. But even if they change them, they have to go through a period of rebellion during which they see themselves as fundamentally different from their parents. Third, in a complex society such as our own, the various sub-social groups have standards of behavior which give prestige and its opposite to its members. If one becomes sufficiently abstract, one can generalize about some of these standards, as when someone points out that gangsters are loyal to their gang and patriots loyal to their country and thus both patriots and anti-social groups are loyal. But clearly the question is not that of loyalty but of that to which one is loyal. And it is the latter which causes the ethical problem to be raised, not the former. Fourth, though there have been times when certain forms of fine arts have been more practised than others, yet there has been no time when there has not been some diversity in these arts. Thus we may say that the thirteenth century was the century of architecture, but it was also the century of literature and sculpture. In the nineteenth century in England, music was not the dominant art—though there was of course English music at that time—but there was nevertheless a good bit of painting and architecture. Leaving aside the question of what need the fine arts satisfy, it is clear that there would not be a variety of arts, if there were not a variety of needs. It is obvious that our architectural needs cannot be satisfied by music nor our musical needs by sculpture. But similarly in the art of living, we cannot satisfy our economic needs by giving ourselves over entirely to warfare or agriculture, for that matter.

The philosopher might be expected to recognize these facts, for they are facts, and to see his problem as that of providing an intellectual framework into which all these activities may be organized. What we ask of the philosopher is not a program of action but a program of understanding. We do not ask him to show us how to make all men into soldiers or farmers or painters, but to show us how all these and other diverse activities can be fitted into a scheme which makes sense. "Sense" does not depend on simplification through extermination. It depends on showing the reason for things. In the days of Maximus of Tyre writers used to discuss the relative merits of rural and urban life, as in the days of Leonardo da Vinci they discussed the relative merits of painting and sculpture. There was supposed to be something called a higher order which would determine the ranks of our activities. But I doubt whether much light is thrown on human behavior by applying the metaphor of the hierarchy any longer. We have still a hierarchy of power and a hierarchy of prestige, but a hierarchy of values, in the sense that some values are lower than others, seems a bit absurd in a civilization which daily is coming to recognize the growing importance of cooperation *versus* competition. Even the most fervent believers in economic competition, it will be noted, also are believers in the right and the duty of competitors to organize for their own protection against foreign competition, taxation, and organized labor, and are loudest in their praise of teamwork and *esprit de corps,* most enthusiastic in the formation of service clubs and fraternities, pathetically generous in public charities for those who are no longer poor, but merely underprivileged.

The philosopher then who wishes to study the art of living would first have to study the society in which the art is practised. He would then have to learn how far we can control our behavior by what we call reason, how rapidly the situations which become problematic change, where conflicting interests lead to complete frustration, whether there is or is not a causal dependence between the satisfaction of certain of our interests, how freely one may satisfy one's drives, how plural one's society is. Unhappily we know very little about such matters and our guide is unexamined custom for the most part. But the encouraging feature of the present is that such questions are considered seriously and for that reason a philosopher is only too happy to raise them.

III

THE ARTS AND CONTEMPORARY LIFE

BY

ALBERT HOFSTADTER

I

The title assigned for this discussion is susceptible of several inter-pretations. It may be taken as an invitation to consider how the arts reflect or fail to reflect present conditions of existence, or in what directions they seem to be proceeding, or the different ways in which they have influenced and been influenced by the experiences of our century. I have taken the liberty, however, of interpreting it in the context of philosophical esthetics. My question will be, *What can the arts do for contemporary man?* The relation between the arts and contemporary life which I shall want to talk about, then, is one of service: *How can art serve man today?*

To this question there are, of course, many answers. For the arts are capable of discharging many functions. They may afford pleasure, amusement, and relaxation; they may provide opportunities for vicarious experience and wish-fulfilment; they may act as an outlet for repressed desires, aggressions, and hostilities; through them we may escape from the harsh realities of the present, and through them we may equally protest against contemporary injustice and evil; in them we may achieve the expression of our selves, our ideals, our visions and faiths, but also by their means we propagandize, advertise, edify. The arts can serve man in all these ways and more. They can perform these functions because they can arouse innumerable forms of mental and spiritual response to a presented world. Men by nature respond in such ways, in one way to the art of Rodgers and Hammerstein, in another to that of Mickey Spillane, in another to that of T. S. Eliot.

Our question needs particularizing. Let us not ask indiscriminately what art can do for us, as it is so obvious that it can do so many things. Let us rather ask particularly, *Is there anything of really fundamental importance that art, and art alone, can do for us?* Is it possible for us today, at this time of tense questioning, in this place of swift violence, to take art seriously? Can art be for us something more than a matter of Friday night opera-going or Saturday afternoon museum-visiting? If we are to speak of the service of art, we must ask how far the arts can go, what serious, important, great thing they can do.

What art can do is related to what we most need. And to the question what contemporary man needs most, there can be but one answer. He needs orientation. He needs, that is, a vital center of devotion, loyalty, effort, and understanding; a structure of meaningfulness adequate to accommodate all aspects of life; a moral and spiritual focus of attraction and authority; a way, in short, of answering life's basic problems, of good and evil, of the finitude of man, of death and life, of destiny. This need for orientation is twofold. On the one hand, we need to achieve a vision of the life and death of man in the world which can be believed, understood, possessed by us. On the other hand, the beliefs and values which go to make up such a vision must be established in our hearts and ways. They must receive vitality, be actualized as forces. Vitality impregnated and justified by meaning and value, meaning and value sustained and effectuated by vitality— this is orientation. It has sometimes also been called authority. But the authority of which I speak is one in free men, individually and in relation, not one exercised over slaves from without.

Another way of putting the matter is to say that the most acute problem facing contemporary men is that of achieving an adequate life-form, both singly and together. We hear often that our age is one of crisis, of insecurity and anxiety. These are symptoms of basic shifts in our culture, on a worldwide scale. We do not have a firm grip on what we are or where we are going. The life of contemporary man is a confirmation of Heraclitus's view of reality as a struggle to maintain form in the flux, integrity and meaning in the passage of events. The stability which constitutes being, he saw, is dependent on measure achieved, on a dynamic equilibrium, like that of the flame maintaining itself through the passage of its materials. When the equilibrium is upset, the process starts anew to re-establish form—not necessarily the same form, but one adapted to the situation, the new conditions and circumstances. The life of the twentieth century has been one involving just this kind of struggle: to achieve a form it lacks. Its conflicts and wars show by their nature the kind of struggle it is: an absolute one, characteristic of an age of total, rather than simply political or religious or economic, transformation.

But the achievement of a life-form is the same as the achievement of orientation or authority. For life-form *is* vital power sustaining ideals and ideals guiding that power; it is the effective interrelation of vitality and meaning. What contemporary men need, then, whether we call it by one name or another, is the ability to make a meaningful response to existence which is of sufficient scope to enlist all of life in its service and of sufficient validity to fructify all of life. The recognition of this need and the search to fulfil it form the burden not only of the serious philosophy of our time, but also of its serious literature —Joyce, Mann, Huxley, Woolf, Eliot, Yeats, Kafka. As Eugene O'Neill wrote to George Jean Nathan: "The playwright of today must dig at the roots of the sickness of today as he feels it—the death of the old God and the failure of science and materialism to give any satisfactory new one for the surviving primitive, religious instinct to find a meaning for life in, and to comfort its fears of death with." [1]

What can the arts do to help us here? That is our particular question.

II

Let us begin by asking whether art is *sufficient* to solve this problem of life-form.

Art would be sufficient if it were able of itself to constitute the meaning of life. If the imaginative life of art, the life of devotion to beauty or esthetic excellence, were the end of all human existence,

---

[1] Quoted in *Literary History of the United States,* The Macmillan Company, New York, revised edition, 1953, p. 1246.

alone giving value to all else, then art would suffice as a solution. This was the doctrine of the Art for Art's Sake school, but its influence spreads wider. One finds the hint of it, for example, in two of the most perfect of Yeats's shorter poems, "Sailing to Byzantium" and "Byzantium." In these the poet contrasts youth with old age, sense with intellect and spirit, time with eternity, vitality with form, and finds the image of the second of each pair in the golden bird, the artificial nightingale:

> Once out of nature I shall never take
> My bodily form from any natural thing,
> But such a form as Grecian goldsmiths make
> Of hammered gold and gold enamelling
> To keep a drowsy Emperor awake;
> Or set upon a golden bough to sing
> To lords and ladies of Byzantium
> Of what is past, or passing, or to come.[2]

It is doubtful whether Yeats himself would have assented to such a doctrine as final truth, however; and in any event, the doctrine cannot be accepted. The merest instance of actual living experience dismisses it, for if it were true, then values of a distinctly non-esthetic nature would surrender their autonomy to esthetic value, and would have become only materials for esthetic purposes. The moral obligation to love my neighbor (as myself, for he is as myself) would be obligatory only because it is justified in some esthetic context, because it contributes in some way to beauty or esthetic excellence. But this cannot be so, for when I experience the obligation to love my neighbor, I experience that love as right and morally compelling without regard to any esthetic function it may have. And we sometimes do, after all, have ugly duties.

To put the matter generally, if art were the meaning of existence, if the esthetic life were human salvation, then the moral life would be denied its native authority and made subservient to the search for esthetic fulfilment. But our experience of morality denies this sub-

[2] W. B. Yeats, "Sailing to Byzantium," *The Collected Poems of W. B. Yeats,* The Macmillan Company, New York, 1951, p. 192, quoted with the permission of the publisher.

servience. Hence art cannot be the meaning of existence. And art cannot, therefore, solve the problem of life-form in this way.

III

But if art cannot itself *be* the meaning of life, is it not the *source* of life's meaning? Must we not go to the artist to get the *raison d'être* of life? We have been told that this is just what we must do by one of the most eminent literary critics and esthetic philosophers of our time, I. A. Richards. Mr. Richards recognized in this book the problem of meaninglessness in modern culture, describing it as "a sense of desolation, of uncertainty, of futility, of the groundlessness of aspirations, of the vanity of endeavor, and a thirst for a life-giving water which seems suddenly to have failed"; these were the signs in consciousness, he said, of a necessary reorganization of our lives. And his solution to it, following Matthew Arnold, lay in poetry:

Our protection . . . is in poetry. It is capable of saving us, or, since some have found a scandal in this word, of preserving us or rescuing us from confusion and frustration. The poetic function is the source, and the tradition of poetry is the guide, of the supra-scientific myths. "The poetry of a people takes its life from the people's speech and in turn gives life to it; and represents its highest point of consciousness, its greatest power and its most delicate sensibility." So wrote the best poet of my generation recently.[3]

That best poet was T. S. Eliot. But Mr. Richards failed to add that in the same book in which Eliot said that he also said:

For Arnold the best poetry supersedes both religion and philosophy. I have tried to indicate the results of this conjuring trick elsewhere. The most generalized form of my own view is simply this: that nothing in this world or the next is a substitute for anything else; and if you find that you must do without something, such as religious faith or philosophic belief, then you must just do without it. I can persuade myself, I find, that some of the things I can hope to get are better worth having than some of the things I cannot get; or I may hope to alter myself so as to

[3] Quoted in Melvin Rader, *A Modern Book of Esthetics, an anthology,* Henry Holt & Company, New York, revised edition, 1952, pp. 299–300.

want different things; but I cannot persuade myself that it is the same desires that are satisfied, or that I have in effect the same thing under a different name. . . . To ask of poetry that it give religious and philosophic satisfaction, while deprecating philosophy and dogmatic religion, is of course to embrace the shadow of a shade.[4]

Were time available, it would be interesting to examine Mr. Richards's attempt to prove that poetry supersedes religion and philosophy. I must content myself, however, with several general remarks.

What could it possibly mean to look upon the poetic function as the source of life's wisdom? Does it mean that what is excellent as poetry is thereby excellent as a guide to the perplexed? But this is surely absurd. For poetry—and art in general—is notoriously indiscriminate with regard to the visions it achieves. Eliot's poetry is excellent as poetry. Must I therefore live by the religion that forms its substance? But then, Ezra Pound's poetry is also excellent poetry (by Eliot's testimony as well). Must I therefore also order my life by the theory of Social Credit, Confucianism, hatred of usury and of "international Jewry"?

Mr. Richards would tell us that poetry is the source of life's wisdom not in the sense that one literally believes its ideological content but rather in the sense that, eliminating or suspending belief, one allows its emotional power to unify one's emotions. But even supposing that poetry does unify emotions, how is such a poetic unification (which must not be supposed *a priori* to be identical with a moral or a religious unification) to function as a source of life's wisdom? For what we require to know in life is whether to choose Eliot's Anglo-Catholicism, or Pound's Confucianism, or whatever, including Richards's Poeticism. This choice (like the principles by which one makes it) lies beyond the poetic as such.

Indeed, if poetry were the source of wisdom in the sense that in poetic excellence one finds what wisdom truly is when separated from the element of belief, or pseudo-belief, we should be back again at the position we have already seen reason to abandon, namely, that poetry—or art in general—is itself the life of meaning. For poetic

[4] T. S. Eliot, *The Use of Poetry and the Use of Criticism,* Harvard University Press, Cambridge, Massachusetts, 1933, pp. 106, 111.

excellence would be the standard by which all things would be measured, and we should be violently and inhumanly wrenching morals and religion into the irresponsibility of beauty.

We cannot elevate art to the status of being the source of life's meaning—which would be esthetic idolatry—because, far from art being the source of life's meaning, it is life which is the source of art's meaning. Art is incapable of *producing* the answers to our problems in so far as it is only art. It can help us in the endeavor to find them, and it can express them as we have found them; but the finding of them is a matter of vital struggle with the problems.

The development of this point brings us to our major concern: a positive statement of the way in which art can be of aid in dealing with contemporary man's problem of meaningful response to his world.

IV

There are two factors involved in the meaningful activity of human beings which we need to consider. One is frequently called "realization"; the other I shall call "congruent response."

By realization we refer to the act of grasping, thinking, apprehending, being aware of something vividly, concretely, in an immediate manner, not in a merely external, verbal, and symbolic manner. To realize something is to "get" it, to have it "come home" to you, to be in possession of it. It is frequently necessary to experience something in order to be able to realize it. Thus visitors to New York seldom realize what its summer climate is like, no matter how much they are told about it, until they suffer it for themselves. People seldom realize that the sum of the interior angles of a triangle equals 180 degrees unless they actually go through the proof with intuitive insight into each step. This last illustration shows, by the way, that even in matters of abstract intellectual knowledge one can attain realization.

On the whole, though, realization is not a matter of intellect alone. It is not a matter of mere cool intellectual understanding or even of vivid intuitive insight, except where the object requires nothing more. In matters of persons, values, qualities, and the like, it is a living, vital, dynamic, immediate grasp of the object, using all the capacities of soul required to grasp that object. No empathy may be required to realize the geometrical theorem, but much is required to realize Hamlet.

As Hamlet does not exist, one can realize non-existent objects. One can also realize falsehoods. It is possible to realize the superiority of white men to Negroes even though they have no such superiority; it is possible to realize that the world's woes are due to the usury instituted by international Jewry, even though this is utter fabrication. Realization does not therefore imply truth any more than it implies the existence of its object. One must not confuse the vivacity, warmth, immediacy, or convincingness of a realized object or proposition with its truth or reality, on pain of admitting that, because Americans are realized by Soviet theatergoers as villains plotting for atomic war, therefore we are in fact villains.

By congruent response I mean a response to a realized object in accordance with how one realizes it. A congruent response is a response which is, as it were, "geared to" a realized object. Such a response includes psychical attitudes, emotions, beliefs, thoughts, and the like, as well as overt behavior. Realizing New York's summer climate, I dread it, desire to escape it, think over how to accomplish this end, and make preparations for removing myself from it. Or again, having violated the law and realizing what I have done, I may feel remorseful or jubilant, depending upon my attitude toward society and its laws; and having one or other of these emotions, I act accordingly.

Just as realization need not be truthful, so a response, to be congruent to the object as realized, need only be directed intentionally toward that object; it need not be a morally right, or a rationally prudent, or a religiously appropriate response. The exultation of the unrepentant sinner over his sin, the sadistic brutality of the criminal who is perfectly aware of his crime, the irrational reaction of the neurotic to a normal situation—all these responses are congruent, for they are directed intentionally toward the object as it is realized. Thus similarly, when two persons hear the same joke, one may be genuinely amused and the other pained, even though both realize it, *i.e.,* get the point of the joke; so that the laughter of the one and the groans of the other are both congruent, both responses to the joke in accordance with the manner of realization of it.

To act meaningfully is to respond congruently to a realized object, situation or problem. (For brevity's sake let us use the word, "object," to stand for all such things.) Hence the ability of man to act meaningfully depends in the first place on his ability to realize what confronts him. No one can make an authentic moral response to a situation involving persons and values without a realization (not simply a report or a calculation) of the values involved and of the persons and their relationships. No one can make an authentic esthetic response to great music without a realization of its expressive form and the values therein embodied. This is true for any field of human concern. It is, therefore, of primary importance for the life of men that they should be able to realize. Indeed one might strongly argue that one large part of the function of education in a free society lies in the task of developing the powers of realization of the student; at least, this is one of the fundamental tasks in liberal education.

The ability of man to act meaningfully depends also on his ability to respond to realized objects with congruent emotions, attitudes, feelings, beliefs, choices, and overt actions. I would stress particularly the aspects of feeling, desire, purpose, and attitude, because they are the motivating factors in human action. Inability to feel, to choose, to decide, to attain to a purpose, to adopt an attitude, are symptoms of failure to achieve the status of a being capable of meaningful life-behavior, failure, therefore, to achieve personality.

These two abilities, to realize and to respond congruently, are not automatically connected. Realizing an object does not automatically evoke a given congruent response. For the response is an act of the person, the whole being, to his realized object, and one cannot point to a unique reflexlike connection between the object as realized (stimulus) and an isolated response to it. The same man may on different occasions make very different responses congruent to similar objects similarly realized. The criminal does not have to see his crime in a new light in order to be remorseful rather than jubilant. He may have so changed in personality that, confronting the same act similarly realized, he now blames himself for what he earlier praised himself.

The combination of such a realizing confrontation of an object and a congruent response to it makes what may be called "an experience." Meaningful human action consists of such experiences; and the engaging in experiences in this sense is human life as the actuality of human capacity for life.

Moreover, such experiences are not only life-acts; they are also experiments in the way of living, for it is only by experience that one comes to realize a particular mode of response to a particular kind of object. The possibility of my realizing love or hatred is given to me by my having engaged in the love or hatred of someone. Knowledge of myself, in the sense of realizing myself, cannot be gained by any method other than experience.

In such experiences, together with the experience of their consequences, we in fact *test* the validity of our mode of life. Only in our confrontations with objects, as persons committed to congruent responses, and as embracing therewith the experiential consequences of our acts, are we brought to realization of what we are, what we are committed to, what we must endure, in the path we have chosen.

Because experiences are actual pieces of living they are real. They constitute and affect our lives. We cannot escape from them. They leave their mark in us and the world. We are responsible for them.

When we look at the problem of life-form or orientation from this standpoint, it becomes the problem of developing a coherent pattern of congruent response to a realized world, including a realized self. It is a problem not only of being able to make one or other kind of congruent response to one or other kind of realized object, but of being able to make a congruent response to the world and what is in it, which shall include the necessary variety of responses to the variety of realized elements that go to make up the world. And above all, it is a problem of developing a pattern according to which we find ourselves able and willing to live, in short, one that is valid, and that proves itself so in the actual living.

This is a problem of philosophy and religion, and as we know has received a large number of solutions in the history of man. The Stoic way of life, the Christian way of life, the Communist way of life are all ways of comprehensive realization and congruent response to the world and what is in it. The validity of such a life-form, as I have said before, can be tested only in actual confrontation by and congruent response to realized objects. In such experience we are brought to realize what we are, what is our chosen destiny, according to that particular life-form. And only such experience can finally tell us whether we can in fact live by and can will to live by that life-form. Accordingly, every experience is essentially serious, however light-hearted or comical it be, and entails a risk proportionate to its nature.

V

These are the necessary preliminaries, and we may now turn directly to the contribution of the arts to the problem of life-form. While art cannot solve that problem by itself as art, it is able to contribute toward a solution because of its unique power of *evoking imaginative experience*. Because of this power of art, men find in the arts a means of stimulation and development of the spirit which is not otherwise afforded, and which provides for the human spirit the analogue of experiment and hypothesis in the sciences. The arts give us experiences that allow us to bring our spiritual powers into exercise. Through them we learn to realize our world and our self, and are thereby given the opportunity to form modes of congruous response to them. That in brief is how the arts can serve toward the achievement of life-form; and we may now consider their function more closely.

VI

"A work of art," said Zola, "is an aspect of creation seen through the medium of a temperament." And with this he formulated succinctly the subject-object structure of artistic realization, for realization is no merely neutral presence of an object to a disembodied intellect, but the grasp of an object by a person, through the powers of personality. It is consciousness in its vital form of concrete and vivid apprehension by means of feeling, attitude, and emotion, as well as perception and thought. The result is that these various dimensions of consciousness, the "subjective" dimensions, are as necessary for the realized presence of the object as, on the other hand, the presence of the object is necessary for the presence of the subject's feelings, emotions, and attitudes.

> Ash on an old man's sleeve
> Is all the ash the burnt roses leave.
> Dust in the air suspended
> Marks the place where a story ended.
> Dust inbreathed was a house—
> The wall, the wainscot and the mouse.
> The death of hope and despair,
>   This is the death of air.[5]

What is the object here? The air's dust? We are contemplating the dust of air as the symbol and the presence of death. But not death as only a physical cessation of life. Death, rather, as the death of hope and despair. We are trying to come to grips with hope and despair, and with them of all life, for they are the epitome of life; and with this, the inevitable passage and defeat of everything important to man. And in the first place it is necessary to realize that defeat, to make it an authentic object of our consciousness. Therefore the poet writes this stanza. But this object—the defeat of human life, as human life—is realized only through the exploitation of a complex of emotions, feelings, and attitudes expressed in the sounds, rhythms, rhymes of the language and in the sequence of images: of roses turned to ash on an old man's sleeve, of the dust of mice in our nostrils. We can taste and smell despair. But what should we have in the way of an object, if our feelings, hopes, valuations were cut off from use in forming these images, following these rhythms, thinking the thought of the stanza?

Every act of realization possesses this kind of subject-object structure, in which subjective and objective components are so united that neither is possible without the other. This is true not only of art but of all experience. It simply comes to very clear exhibition in art be-

[5] T. S. Eliot, "Little Gidding." *The Complete Poems and Plays,* Harcourt, Brace & Company, New York, 1952, p. 139.

cause art specializes in producing realization. The artist is a man who has the means and the power of realizing and of expressing what he realizes. This means that he is simultaneously a man of sensitivity, talent, and skill, in command of the rhetoric of his medium, and a man of vision and insight, with the power of realization, at the service of which his rhetoric operates. Without the rhetoric, his expression is fumbling; without the realization, he is a mere magician, a trickster, a windbag.

Because realization involves a subjective, as well as an objective, dimension, the work of art is always personal. The artist's insight, vision, realization is always *his,* and our participation in it is therefore a participation in another's experience. Rembrandt's people differ from Van Gogh's, and both from Picasso's, not only in costume, occupation, or other objective particularities, but also and more importantly in the ways in which these artists see, feel, experience people. The differing techniques—Rembrandt's chiaroscuro, Van Gogh's expressionism, Picasso's abstractionism—are not only differences in rhetoric, but differences in realization. They are different means of expressing the qualities of people realized by the artists.

For this reason, the arts enable us to participate in another's experience. It is almost literally true that through art we pass out of ourselves and into the spiritual orientation of other selves. This is an extremely important element in the service of art; for not only is art, as Dewey said, the freest form of communication between men, but it is the most powerful means we have of sharing the best of the experiences of the most sensitive and sincere of men.

Art, then, through its power of realization, wakens our spirit from the slumber of ordinary existence, raises it to a level of vital consciousness of which it would have been incapable by itself, and at the same time enables it to participate with others in their objects and modes of vision.

VII

Because art is a most powerful means of realization, it is also a floodgate capable of releasing our powers of spiritual response. A good joke, well told, invites us to laughter. A good tragedy, well produced, invites us to more than can be said in a few words: the catharsis of fears and anxieties, communion with men in a common destiny, humbling of pride, victory over triviality, detachment from the merely personal, dedication to the good despite every terror of existence— these are but a few of the functions which have been assigned to tragedy.

We cannot make a meaningful response, act in a meaningful human way, except to an object according to the way in which we realize it. And conversely, according to the way in which we realize an object, *we have the opportunity to create a response.* If I am confronted by a terrifying beast, I shall fear and run. If I am confronted by a saint, I shall revere and adore. But how shall I be confronted by either? I must realize them as beast or saint. This done, it is open to me to fear or revere. So it is with all significant human experience. *The opportunity to perform a spiritual act, to exercise the human spirit, is given by, and given only by, realization of an object appropriate to that kind of act.* How shall I be able to summon up the spiritual courage necessary to face and deal with myself as hollow and my world as without sense if I cannot envision myself or the world as such? Who among us has been able to achieve that vision, and thereby the opportunity to respond to it spiritually? Here lies the use of Kafka or Eliot, without whom many of us would be as innocent babes.

Art, thus, working through its power of realization, has the power of *evocation;* it calls the human spirit to make an appropriate response to an object which is of concern to it. And here, too, participation with others is of great importance. To laugh with others, to weep with others, over the same object, is to engage in a community of feeling and response without which men are inhuman. Art, by making this possible, is one of the few bridges extending between man and man.

VIII

Behind the power of realization which makes spiritual evocation possible, is the power of imagination which makes realization possible. The word, "imagination," has had a variety of meanings in the discussion of the arts. I shall mean by it here *the power of employing a medium to achieve a realized object, independently of whether that object actually exists or not.* Thus Thomas Mann uses the medium of language to achieve Hans Castorp, independently of whether that young man actually exists. And when we read *The Magic Mountain* we ourselves are using the language already written there to achieve Hans Castorp as a realized object for us. Both author and reader employ imagination, though in different ways.

Art is essentially imaginative. What distinguishes the arts is the fact that their objects are realized in and through the use of a medium. If there is any general formula definitory of art, I should suppose it to be: *art is the imaginative realization of objects capable of evoking characteristic spiritual responses,* as, for instance, comic art is the imaginative realization of objects with the incongruities required to evoke laughter.

The fact that art is essentially imaginative, that it has the power of realizing chosen objects by the exploitation of a medium, is of importance for understanding art's service because it lies at the basis of the richness, vital economy, and psychical efficiency with which art evokes experience.

Whatever else may be characteristic of the media of the arts, one attribute is supremely significant. A medium is a material with great potentialities for expressive realization. Out of language and its meanings, colors, shapes, musical sounds, it is possible to create suggestions of objects of myriad kinds, whether like those actually existent or different. In the realm of art man is able to exercise a creativity almost analogous to the divine. Out of language and behavior he can fashion a *Cyrano de Bergerac* or an *Oedipus Rex,* out of color and line a *View of Toledo* or a *Guernica* mural, out of musical sound a *Mazurka* or a *St. Matthew Passion.*

This means that on an imaginative level, through the creation of images (of objects realized in and through a medium), rich and wide ranges of possibilities of human experience open up for exploration. The artist, by mastery of his medium, is able to reach and to help us to reach experiences that would otherwise be closed to us. Through them we enter this world, but also worlds that never were nor will be, yet worlds in which we begin to realize the possibilities of meaning in human life: *The Afternoon of a Faun, Tristan and Isolde, Ulysses, The Red Badge of Courage, War and Peace, The Waste Land*. And, as we have seen, realizing such objects also means experiencing appropriate feelings, emotions, and attitudes, and being challenged to make congruent spiritual responses: sympathies and antipathies, choices, wishes, hopes. One cannot be neutral toward Tristan or toward Leopold Bloom. Rather, to them and to their struggles and values one must respond with even greater acuity than toward most of the actual people one knows, just because one realizes them better than the actual people.

A medium is thus a rich mine of human experience. It is also a great economizer of life. In life we can live and die but once; in art, many times, in different ways. The existence of artistic media makes it possible for us to share in and contemplate experiences without paying the inevitable price that actual existence would demand. I cannot murder my beloved out of jealous passion, but I can share in that experience with Othello. I cannot, in the single noble act of my pitiful life commit suicide for the sake of my son, but I can share in that act with Willy Loman. Artistic media are the means whereby the human spirit can experience values and meanings with great economy of human life. This is an inestimable advantage. For, as I have said, it is only in confrontation by and congruent response to realized objects that we can test the validity of a life-form; so that, were we restricted to experiences of actualities, the subject-matter of our spiritual experiments would be disastrously insufficient in scope, and the experiments fatally dangerous in execution.

A medium, finally, is a most efficient device for pure, intense realization. As the artist employs it, the medium consists of stimuli and clues to perception and realization. A few lines on paper instantly convey a face, a few sounds in rhythmic order instantly form a leaping, bounding movement. Thus the artist, manipulating the medium, is able to control and give opportunity to perception. The master of the medium is he who can, by proper and economical selection and ordering of his materials, rouse us to unusual height and penetration of realization. He is able to eliminate everything superfluous, everything accidental, and concentrate on the essentials. He is able to bring the object to us unencumbered with irrelevancies, as life and nature never do.

This makes it possible for us not only to enter strange new worlds but to enter into our own world and our own self as never before. By his very distortions, simplifications, abstractions, violences, the artist can give us a clearer, more vivid, more solid, more expressive vision of what exists than the actual presence of it before us, for ordinary experience is dumb as compared with experience raised by art to the level of intense realization. As Picasso once said, "We all know that art is not truth. Art is a lie that makes us realize truth, at least the truth that is given us to understand."

Art, then, through its imaginative power (through its creation of an image by the use of a medium) is able to give us the realization of things actual, possible and impossible, of the real and the unreal, is able to widen immeasurably the range of human experience and thus to widen equally the range of opportunities of the human spirit to exercise, test, and come to know itself. And art is able to do this in comparative safety and with great economy and efficiency precisely because it is imaginative. In the words of Henry James, ". . . in literature we move through a blest world in which we know nothing except by style, but in which also everything is saved by it, and in which the image is thus always superior to the thing itself," words which are almost identically repeated by the painter Bill Scott in Christopher Isherwood's *Lions and Shadows*, ". . . the pattern evolved from the reality is more important than the reality itself . . ." [6]

IX

Such is the service of art, stemming from its powers of imagination, realization, and evocation and issuing in the formation of rich, varied, personal and interpersonal experience. *Art is the principle of the wakefulness of the spirit.* In it the spirit attains, in the words of Henry James again, "perception at the pitch of passion."

[6] Christopher Isherwood, *Lions and Shadows, An Education in the Twenties,* L. & Virginia Woolf at the Hogarth Press, London, 1938, p. 266.

Yet like all powers, art is ambivalent and has its limitations. As energy may be used either for destructive or for constructive purposes, so may art. Realization may be of the unreal as of the real, of the false as of the true; and response may be evil or irrational while yet congruent to its object. Our realizations may be illusions and the responses which we are prompted to make to them may be acts of spiritual suicide. We may be drugged by the poisonous atmosphere of a falsely realized self and world into the acceptance of a vicious life-form. And the artfulness of art is no cure for such a disease.

It is no cure because the artfulness of art and the truth or validity of its vision are not identical. As an act of imagination, realizing objects in and through a medium, there is a tension within it, the tension between those characteristics which relate to its imaginative nature— the "esthetic" characteristics—and those which relate to the truth, reality, and validity of its objective content. If in *The Waste Land* Eliot attempted to realize the meaninglessness and forsakenness of modern culture, he did this by exploiting sounds, rhymes, rhythms, images, and meanings characteristic of the English language. One can therefore concentrate on his success in the use of the medium and the "esthetic" characteristics of the poem resulting from this: its poetic architecture, the brilliance and variety of the images, the almost musical contrapositions of the sections. All these represent the "kind of consciousness" exhibited in the poem as distinct from the non-esthetic values of the object realized—its truth, for instance, as a realization of modern culture. So a critic who was among the first to recognize Eliot's merits has pointed out that the Anglo-Catholicism in Eliot is one thing and the "modes of feeling, apprehension and expression" another "such as we can find nowhere earlier." And he maintained that Eliot was significant for younger poets "because contemporary poets are likely to find that the kind of consciousness represented by *Ash Wednesday* and *Marina* has a close bearing upon certain problems of their own." [7]

One may also concentrate on the truth of the realization, or on its moral or religious values; and we have no assurance that esthetic per-

[7] F. R. Leavis, *New Bearings in English Poetry*, Chatto & Windus, London, 1942, p. 132.

fection correlates with these other values. Esthetic perfection may consort with falsehood, moral degradation, religious idolatry. And this is what leads to the inner tension of art. For most artists are also men concerned with the problems of men, and hence concerned with values of the ethical, political, religious, as well as esthetic order. One thinks of Giotto, Goya, Daumier, El Greco, Rembrandt, or of Tolstoy, Dante, Mann, of Bach and Beethoven. The artists, too, must risk the choice of values. What is there in Gertrude Stein apart from a virtually complete dominance of esthetic values for their own sake? Whereas in Hemingway, who learned so much from her technically, there has never been an absence of serious concern with life values, whether those of the artist's honesty and integrity in the midst of a shattered world whose only constant certainty is death, or of loyalty, love and solidarity as in *For Whom the Bell Tolls.* What but the deepest attachment to life values leads Robert Penn Warren again and again, as in *Night Rider* and *All the King's Men,* to preoccupation with the problem of evil and of the moral finitude of the individual, or Edwin Arlington Robinson, in his last great poem, *King Jasper,* to offer tribute to love, wisdom, and courage, even when man has to pay for evil with his own life, yet also to exalt life in the greatness of its ability to survive all its protagonists with their human good and evil alike?

The lack of correlation between esthetic and non-esthetic values in art may tempt the artist confronted by a world of brutality, uncertainty, and crumbling values, to seek for spiritual security at least in the domain of esthetic values, in beauty, artifice, fantasy, or in the domain of artistic values, in sincerity, honesty, integrity in the treatment of the medium, as in the cases of James Branch Cabell or Gertrude Stein. It may also tempt him to the opposite extreme, in which he will trumpet with Frank Norris: "Who cares for fine style! . . . We don't want literature, we want life." The result will be works like Richard Wright's *Native Son,* of which R. P. Blackmur has said that it is "one of those books in which everything is undertaken with seriousness except the writing." [8]

[8] Richard P. Blackmur, *The Expense of Greatness,* Arrow Editions, New York, 1940, p. 295.

The first of these extremes—estheticism in art—retains at least the merit of being art, though sometimes at the cost of triviality. The second, by abandoning art, abandons imagination and with it the possibilities of realization and experience that are its offspring. It therefore weakens its capacity to do just what it aims to do, to bring the reader or spectator to a deeprooted awareness of its subject. These are the poles between which art trembles in tension. They represent the two non-identical criteria by which art is judged, the values of art and the values of life.

Both criteria are necessary. It is insufficient to judge art simply as art, simply as an act of imagination. Life will not permit us, nor will reason, to stop there. There is nothing about art as such which guarantees the validity or the importance of the artist's insight into matters human or divine. Artistic success, or perfection, means only success in realization, the success of imagination. But what is realized, what is brought to form in apprehension, is not therefore necessarily valid. The *judgment* as to its truth and importance, and even more significant, the *spiritual retort*—the congruent response—to it when it is so judged, these are no longer matters of the art work, of art, of esthetic value, but of life. They are acts which presuppose the experience of the art work, but they are acts of the spirit which moved beyond imagination as such. They occur at the junctures at which life leaves off being art, however serious great art may be, and becomes something infinitely more serious.

Virginia Woolf's *To The Lighthouse* is generally recognized as her best novel. It embodies her peculiarly lyrical, almost breathlessly delicate technique at its finest. There is no question but that the realization of the characters in the situation is perfect, and that one gets the author's attempted resolution of the problem of meaningfulness in both form and substance of the work. That resolution is stated at one place in the thoughts of Lily Briscoe: the meaning of life lies not in one single truth, but in all the momentary revelations of meaning, in all the momentary stabilities in the flux of life, in the patterns of mutual understanding, of interlocking of things and persons, that emerge momentarily from the endless passage.

What is the meaning of life? That was all—a simple question; one that tended to close in on one with years. The great revelation had never come. The great revelation perhaps never did come. Instead there were little daily miracles, illuminations, matches struck unexpectedly in the dark; here was one. This, that, and the other; herself and Charles Tansley and the breaking wave; Mrs. Ramsay bringing them together; Mrs. Ramsay saying, "Life stand still here"; Mrs. Ramsay making of the moment something permanent (as in another sphere Lily herself tried to make of the moment something permanent)—this was of the nature of a revelation. In the midst of chaos there was shape; this eternal passing and flowing (she looked at the clouds going and the leaves shaking) was struck into stability. Life stand still here, Mrs. Ramsay said. "Mrs. Ramsay! Mrs. Ramsay!" she repeated. She owed it all to her.[9]

All this has been made real to the reader. Yet he has now to judge, now to make the spiritual retort. We have realized this solution. Is it, can it be, ours? The novel cannot answer this question. It cannot assume a responsibility which is ours only. It has served its purpose well in bringing us to the point at which we are able to ask the question, understanding what we mean. But to decide whether it is so, whether we are to accept it, whether we can live by it, whether it can be our faith, no novel and no art suffices, but only the spirit itself, at its own risk and on its own responsibility. Art has dignity enough in conducting us to the point at which this risk and this responsibility can be ours.

[9] Virginia Woolf, *To The Lighthouse,* Harcourt, Brace & Company, New York, 1927, pp. 240–241.

IV

NEW HORIZONS IN THE NOVEL

BY

WILLIAM G. ROGERS

In all the history of this country, there never were so many books, either in number of copies or number of titles. And though there never were simultaneously so many distractions—movie, radio, television, auto ride, even the luncheon speaker—there were never so many book readers. Publishers provide some 9,000 new trade titles yearly, and they sell into the millions. In addition we have multimillions of low-priced reprints, the paper-covered books, of which about 275,000,000, mostly novels, were distributed in 1952 alone. So the written word gets attention.

Whether the writer originates his ideas, or whether they work up automatically into his receptive, trained consciousness out of the constant ferment of his society, he is the key figure in the thought of today, as he was of yesterday, as he will be of tomorrow. He is the inescapable, immovable focus. If we refuse to acknowledge his stature affirmatively, it can be proved, in spite of us, negatively: it is properly measured not only by what we say for him but also by what others say against him.

In the past few years, enemies have directed at him an increasingly stubborn, astute, and virulent attack. They complain of obscenity, or lewdness. Or beating around the bush, they come up with the accusation that the books of a man with a character morally or ideologically reprehensible, as they allege, are not fit to read. These charges appear to be, under thin disguises, actual attacks on freedom of expression. They strike perilously close to the books themselves. The officious, self-appointed censors are smart enough, of course, to understand about killing two birds with one stone. There is only one kind of bad book, ultimately, and one kind of dangerous book. Many of them have appeared recently, too, and one phrase defines them all: the only bad book, the only dangerous book, is the one a man is forbidden to read.

So while books may be considered in some complacent quarters as entertainment, and no more, as "escape," in short, as superficial, they are very seriously regarded by their foes, and consequently must be regarded by their friends as central in our society.

By books I mean of course novels, which is my topic. The novelist, is not necessarily the thinker, though thought is a part of his method and a part of his material. An artist who has been a friend of mine a long time invites me to view his latest oil. He stands rapt before it, and there he exclaims with the utmost sincerity and the utmost conviction:

"What a wonderful picture! It's a masterpiece!"

It sounds like the utmost conceit, too. Yet he is mainly a religious painter, and a devout one, and in his eyes this painting is really not his handiwork at all, but the good Lord's, done not by a master but by the Master. My friend sincerely identifies himself as only the humble tool, the go-between.

To precisely the same extent, the novelist acts as the go-between. The honest novelist without undue immodesty can claim the exalted rank of masterpiece for this or that work of his own. In other words, he alone did not create it, his brain or heart exclusively did not produce it. Somebody or something else had a finger in the pie. He and his time share the paternity. In a real way he just cannot help himself. He's in the groove, as they say, he's on the beam. But the groove was there, the beam was there, they are the unique groove and beam fashioned by his society, made in America. Does his work require brains? Yes, but primarily it requires a rare and curious faculty that may be described as novelistic aptitude. And I suppose novelistic aptitude may be described as a combination of litmus paper, carbon paper, and typewriter paper.

Novels fall into two categories, those that count and those that don't. The latter, barely skin deep, are manufactured, turned out for practical purposes, by a layman. The former come from the creative worker, the consecrated novelist who writes first, eats and sleeps second; no doubt he abhors that chronology, but it is in his blood. These worthwhile, superior novels—they may not attain an acceptable esthetic standard, they merely have to be written in the professional, sublimated spirit—are often by a man who is not a philosopher, nor perhaps even a sound thinker. The long flexible fingers which may produce a distinguished pianist do not necessarily keep him from being a dolt. The right arrangement of gristle, muscle, and open spaces in a throat which may fashion a great singer is not always matched, higher up, by the wit that will teach him to come in out of the rain. A novelist must use brains, he exists many cuts above such a singer or pianist. But brains are not his forte. He's a kind of feeler, a watcher and observer, a participant, maybe, an absorbent something. The day in which he lives provides his sustenance, and he lives in his day even though he lives in an ivory tower.

So as he forms an integral part of his day, his novel forms an integral part of it, too. There is a real sense in which you cannot remove the novel of Balzac from the reign of Louis Philippe, or the novel of Mérimée from the reign of Napoleon III, as you most obviously cannot lift the pretty portraits of Winterhalter from Napoleon's court, or the paintings of Cézanne from his Provence, or the lithographs of Daumier from his Paris. Our novelist cannot be lifted from our day, either. It is a parasitic relationship. Or we may say that he acts as a reflector; or we may regard him as a kind of copycat. For better or worse, we are stuck with him. And no less importantly, he is stuck with us. He must be hoist with our bootstraps if he be hoist at all.

This, roughly, is the process: a groundswell in the land and people that lie at the base of the novelist's existence makes itself felt, drives him to work; and his novel reacts to this lift, is marked with it as the squares of the graph are cut by the zigzag of the seismographic needle. That's his material, it's up to him to make lasting art out of it.

Fifty years from now our most successful novelists may be completely forgotten—I hope a lot of them will be, too. The novelist whose opinions coincide most closely with ours may not outlast his lifetime —that prospect does not disturb me, either. The novelist is not great, or even potentially great, because we agree with him, nor because he handles an apparently important topic, nor is he insignificant because we disagree. In the past quarter century, when dissensions have cut so deeply and left horrible scars, many books have been published with parts of which we all must quarrel. Louis Ferdinand Céline's *Voyage au bout de la nuit,* for example, contains offensive anti-American passages, and the author himself was so flagrantly pro-Fascist that his French countrymen exiled him. Right here at home, a learned, eloquent, and influential poet has championed views which most of us cannot tolerate, and behaved in a manner which the courts label traitorous. I mean Ezra Pound. The opinions of both these men seem to us abominable. They will always seem so. Yet in spite of that, Céline and Pound possess talents so rare they border on genius. They are infinitely superior to many writers whose vast popular successes are scored in part because they do think as we want them to think, because they are intellectually obliging, so to speak. That is not to be intellectual at all, of course; that in effect is to write out of the harmless and static areas of living where indeed no living goes on.

The novelist owes his greatness to the fundamental, unpredictable, inscrutable needs he satisfies. You can measure this greatness, it is utilitarian; prosaically, he earns his keep through the ages, or he fails to. He is great by the decision of the finicky future, which will pick and choose, without any by-your-leave, the most unaccountable matters from the present. He is great by virtue of incommensurable qualities like intensity, or by virtue of supreme control of his medium, or because of something that persists in staying alive in his pages. I am feeling around for a working definition of the nature of genius. Or I may put it this way: if I knew what twenty-first century man could not get along without, I could list every present novelist who will survive. Writers do not last out of the past purely because they said something worth saying, however; it was also because they said it memorably, though to be sure, the two, right content and right style, often go together. In other words, while time may weed out the thought, the stuff, the idea, it cannot eliminate the first rate talent. The one living thing that cannot be killed is the living book.

Specifically who is the novelist today? We will never live long enough to learn for sure. Without the aid of the essential perspective, however, we take the chance of naming a few names.

Novels may be classified in a lot of ways: good, bad, or indifferent; romantic or realistic; best sellers or failures; by topic, such as war, labor, politics, love, and so on; or by author, such as man, woman, Baptist, ex-Communist, ex-Baptist. I would like to make use of a jumbled classification, one which perhaps needs an apology but which is going to get merely an explanation. As no hard and fast division covers the whole field, I resort to a natural division, I take novels as they come, as they occur not to the scholar, perhaps, but to the bookstore browser. Despite some overlapping, the advantages of these groups are that they are familiar, workable and not forced.

Let us begin with the best publicized efforts to outguess the future— the system of prizes and awards. Is the novelist with the new message which we are seeking the prize winner? Sinclair Lewis, Pearl Buck, and William Faulkner have won Nobel literary prizes. National Book Awards have been bestowed on Nelson Algren, James Jones, Ralph Ellison, and Faulkner again. Among recipients of Pulitzers in the past fifteen years there are James Gould Cozzens, Martin Flavin, Ellen Glasgow, A. J. Guthrie, Jr., Ernest Hemingway, John Hersey, John P. Marquand, James A. Michener, Margaret Mitchell, Marjorie Kinnan Rawlings, Conrad Richter, John Steinbeck, Upton Sinclair, Robert Penn Warren, Herman Wouk.

Some of these men and women, for instance, Hemingway and Lewis, were writing a quarter of a century ago. Novelists so long established will not offer anything new for tomorrow that they have not already offered for today; they have not been holding out on us. We are concerned with the present, our present, the 1950's, or at least the past eight or ten years. Within this time limit, do these writers, do any of them, does any one of them, wave us on toward "new horizons"? Do they supply fresh insights into our times? Do they summon us to support a cause which had not gained our allegiance before? Is there an increased intensity? Do they speak with an eloquent new tongue, as their predecessors did in the 1920's?

Mindful always of our concern with the immediate present, with a new indebtedness and not one old and previously acknowledged, I answer, "no."

I revere many of these names, but for the same reasons for which I revered them twenty-five years ago. And if I am reluctant to pronounce a blanket "no" on them all, as of today, it is because I remember how easily I err. To test my judgment, then, I turn to some other period for a basis of comparison. Let us look back just a century. Fresh off the presses came what we must call, without fear of challenge, the flower of our country's letters: Herman Melville's *Moby Dick* and Nathaniel Hawthorne's *The House of the Seven Gables,* both 1851, and other Melville and Hawthorne before and after. The stature of this immortal fiction and this memorable period looms all the larger when we include other contemporary works. It was in the 1850's that Thoreau wrote *Walden,* Whitman, *Leaves of Grass,* and Emerson, *Conduct of Life.*

Whether novels, poetry, or essays, they are all truly creative and imaginative. You may question, charitably, whether we have a right to require our writer today to be a Melville or a Hawthorne. The answer must be, that we allow no writer to be anything less. We look up to the writer not because he is pretty good but because he is great, or at least potentially great. We hope some of these contemporaries of ours, before they die, will become no less great. But as of the moment, they, and their books, too, lack something.

But still, you protest, the 1850's are remote, and rose to a formidable peak. Let us turn to an intermediate area for comparative purposes. Let us look briefly at a period we know firsthand. If it is unjust to match today's novelist against the champions, what about setting him up against the finest to appear in this century?

The 1920's open auspiciously with F. Scott Fitzgerald's *This Side of Paradise.* In 1921, came Edith Wharton's *The Age of Innocence,* Sinclair Lewis's *Main Street,* John Dos Passos's *Three Soldiers,* and Sherwood Anderson's *The Triumph of the Egg.* In 1922, there were Lewis's *Babbitt,* and E. E. Cummings's *The Enormous Room.* Notice these other significant dates: 1925, Theodore Dreiser's *An American Tragedy,* Fitzgerald's *The Great Gatsby,* Lewis's *Arrowsmith,*

Anderson's *Dark Laughter;* 1926, Hemingway's *The Sun Also Rises;* 1929, Hemingway's *Farewell to Arms,* Faulkner's *The Sound and the Fury,* and Thomas Wolfe's *Look Homeward, Angel.* It is relevant to point out that everybody in all creative fields kept busy with pen, pencil, and brush. In the single decade, to mention random items, Gershwin composed *Rhapsody in Blue* and the *Piano Concerto;* Aaron Copland write his *First Symphony;* from Hart Crane we had *White Buildings* and from T. S. Eliot, *The Waste Land.*

All that furious creative activity boiled and bubbled within twelve years after the close of World War I. Eight years have passed since World War II. It is fair, then to check one period against the other. What we find today suffers by the comparison. It is not only that we lack a *Moby Dick* and *Seven Gables;* we also lack *This Side of Paradise, Main Street, Three Soldiers, An American Tragedy,* and so on.

So if we confine ourselves to prize winners, they come off second best; the prizes belong in the 1920's, not in the 1950's. Prize winners, however, often bear an academic taint, and formal rewards mark rather a past service than a future promise. Let us hunt some more. There used to be, three or four decades ago, a very choice hidingplace for talent—and hidingplace it was, considering the few readers who looked there. It was *transition* and *This Quarter* and other publications founded and edited for the experimenter. He showed up there, too: James Joyce, Gertrude Stein, and others who foreshadowed the writing to come, and to stay. Today New Directions supplies a welcome anthology of "new" writing. Several reprint houses have ventured understandingly into a field vacated by the hardcover but timid and, so to speak, softshell publishers. There have been Edwin Seaver's yearly *Cross Section* and Dorothy Norman's *Twice A Year.* Excellent quarterlies still exist.

But the open arms of the most openminded editors are empty gestures if no one is doing brand new writing. They broadcast invitations to a splendid party, but nary a guest shows up. Despite their earnest, diligent search, they have not found writing that can be labeled pioneering, that tells us the recognizable but hitherto unsuspected truths, what we knew but had not yet learned, what we accept the instant we see it but cannot formulate for ourselves, what was right there though without help we could not put our finger on it.

What other groups must we look into? I would like right here to dismiss one small but influential set of novelists. They are the extremists, the do-or-die novelists, who scream to force you to listen. They have earned a respectable audience, and are by all means serious. They are too serious. They try to write bigger and blacker than the headlines. Some younger writers have adopted, especially within the past two or three years, such strained subjects, such unnatural and inhuman subjects as drug addicts and peddlers, baby killers, patricides, driveling idiots, the man who murders a priest with a crucifix, the tough guy who with fists or gun butt pounds his victim to a jelly, a pulp, a mash—the popular technique requires grisly details. This school of writing has hooked other dupes, too, or at least has set up a sort of annex. The author of the longest novel ever published in the United States belongs among these attention-getters.

Great literature is not stunts, nor is it abnormalities, of which indeed there are fewer than some novelists pretend. The world is not composed exclusively of the pervert, the insane, the incestuous; there never were such unrelieved Gothic horrors. These extremists fail because of their lack of a sense of proportion; they forget that there were exactly as many wise as foolish virgins. Many of our writers treat the usual and the familiar, the topic with which we all rub elbows, that touches us on all sides, not the journalistic topic, that hits us between the eyes, that shouts from the rooftops.

The commonest single subject in the past ten or twelve years has been the soldier and the sailor, or the family that sacrifices a boy or girl to the war, or the girl the soldier left behind—or girls. I hardly need name James Jones, Norman Mailer, Herman Wouk, James A. Michener, Louis Falstein, Irwin Shaw, John Horne Burns.

The novelist has been discussing the adolescent, too. Some of our most original and rewarding stories deal with youth in crisis. Among them are Truman Capote's *Other Voices, Other Rooms,* Carson McCullers's *The Member of the Wedding,* and J. M. Salinger's *The Catcher in the Rye.*

There also has been important regional fiction: Harriet Arnow's *Hunter's Horn,* Feike Feikema's *The Chokecherry Tree* and *This Is the Year,* Jessamyn West's *The Friendly Persuasion,* Henry Hornsby's *Lonesome Valley,* Carlyle Tillery's *Red Bone Woman,* Byron Herbert Reece's *Better a Dinner of Herbs.*

And they write, as they always will and always must, about social problems, about the status of labor, the relation of the Jew to his Gentile community, the hardship of being a Negro. The best novel in fifteen years on the race question—some would call it the best novel in fifteen years—concerned South Africa, of course, instead of America. It was Alan Paton's *Cry, the Beloved Country,* almost unendurably tender and touching. This vital racial topic, even though it seemed to have little interest for big sections of our book-buying public, inspired some able American talents. Chester Himes's *If He Hollers Let Him Go* was a fine, unpopular but savage outcry against the injustice which plagues Negroes, and Ann Petry's *The Street* stressed the pathos and tragedy not only of the Negro but also by implication of any slum dweller regardless of color. Jefferson Young's *A Good Man* described a Negro who longed, too naively, to ape the white man's ways. There was also *The Plantation,* by Ovid Williams Pierce, about the love of man for place, and of man for man, and how a skimping of it can hurt mercilessly.

But by now both the Young and the Pierce remove us a little from the problem novel. We have shifted rather toward a general picture of the American scene. One of the most noteworthy examples of it, and one of the year's best novels, was Mark Harris's *The Southpaw,* as adult as Ring Lardner and somehow fresher. There are other names to remember, such as Wright Morris, Louis Auchincloss, Saul Bellow.

Why cannot we help the novelist out and, frankly, select essential topics for him—for example, baseball? We pay more attention to newsy things than he does; we have time, perhaps, or they matter more, or we think they matter more. Isn't he always digging out something that does not seem of first importance? For instance, the Civil War was thirty years old before he got around to doing a masterpiece, Stephen Crane's *The Red Badge of Courage.* That appeared about the time of the Spanish-American War, which has not inspired any masterpiece at all as yet. Suppose we offer suggestions. In July, 1953, for example, we should have urged him, at the start of the month, to tackle the tragedy of war, as in Korea; but by the end of the month that topic would have been outmoded, would have been dropped from page one, and we should have assigned him in its place the blessings of peace. Under Democratic administrations we should expect him to write about social legislation; under Republican, about individual initiative. Conversely, we would have been glad to have him skip the depression, which somehow showed the nation in a bad light. In spite of us, he did a very sound book on it, while his painter friends, incidentally, much to the distress of some art lovers, insisted on immortalizing on canvas or in lithograph and silk-screen print the breadline, and the bum poking through the refuse barrel for clothing or food.

Assignment and suggestion are utterly impossible. We do not know enough. The novelist's decision is forced on him by that groundswell, by an indefinable something under our feet, or in the air, it is not so simple as baseball, or Korea, political rivalry, depression. Nor is it so journalistic. Nor is it so obvious.

A book designer confided to me, some months ago, that in working out an illustration for a novel about a Negro, he painstakingly left his hero nondescript, neither black nor white, in the jacket picture which would first catch the public eye on a bookstore counter. Why? Though he and the publisher, too, recognized the theme as timely and worthy, they suspected some readers were sated with it, and would prefer something new rather than another version of the already familiar story about racial prejudice.

There is nothing new about problems, particularly about our problems, whether international rivalry, religious or sectional intolerance, or even love, a trouble so old and so new. What we want, if I may say so, is more problems. At least we want something on which we have not freshly exercised our imaginations. Nothing is settled, and it would be unthinkable to neglect the prejudice and intolerance, or even the heartache of love. Yet the flighty, undependable, and shameless emotions can, much as we disapprove, reach an exhaustion point. The time comes when, beyond our control, they are practically forced to relax even their most solemn commitments. The time comes when we are fed up, as the saying goes. People sometimes are fed up worthily with the horrors of war, sometimes disgracefully with the bounties of peace. For us today, old problems remain unsolved, new problems are still indistinct. The novelist has no use for the one, cannot yet get his hands on the other. He cannot help himself, we cannot help him; he lacks a new subject and cannot invent anything new to do with the old. Old wine in new bottles, new wine in old bottles—either combination would work for him, but he cannot manage either.

If he cannot help himself, it is because in part we are not helping him. What after all is really new about our time? The writer of the 1920's, whom we today still find relevant, had the good fortune to step upon the threshold of another age, different according to the indisputable evidence of the overwhelming facts—and this is not to ignore Dreiser, Crane, London at the turn of the century. Do we, in 1953, have something new in the rewarding and fruitful sense in which newness existed a quarter century ago, let alone half a century? We are stuck with the writer, as I said before; and I also said, he is stuck with us. He can be no better than we are, or no better than we allow or oblige him to be. Where do we learn about the new American truth? From the novelist. Where does he learn about it? From us. Remember the question, which comes first, chicken or egg? In creative writing, they come together. What the novelist invents, and what he imagines, grow out of the times he lives in, his times and ours. For instance, we have long been anticipating, whenever we opened a war novel, the so-called "great" World War II novel. It is not here yet. It may be too early. It may also be, and this seems more plausible, that we already have the great World War II novel in Hemingway's great World War I *Farewell to Arms*. Does the new war differ so much from the old? Isn't it still a part of the same age? Isn't it the same groundswell? And is the rest of the truth about us now in 1953 just the old familiar 1920's truth but worn and dulled and diminished?

What other experiences, and vistas, besides war, have we provided for the novelist? What can he do with the great gifts of the atomic age? The only thing he has done so far is science fiction, which is worse than nothing. The fact is that we at large do not ask much of him. We suggest no challenge to him. Instead of counting on him, we count on the psychiatrist, or the physicist. Think for how many good novels a Kinsey report is a pedantic substitute! When the novelist accomplishes something worthwhile, we honor him with a medal which unwise distribution has somewhat tarnished. When he offends, we accuse him and his book of lewdness and obscenity, and for good measure we ask him whether his wife's second cousin didn't, in 1936, attend a meeting at which the chairman belonged to an anti-Fascist organization which a Legion post in California has declared to be a Communist front outfit? In other words, if we have not forfeited all rights to a Melville, a Hawthorne, a new Hemingway, a new Wolfe, we have done ridiculously little to prepare for one.

In one respect we give our novelist a great deal: A country possessed of enormous military power, master of incredible production facilities, builder of unparalleled networks of roads and television cables, blessed with matchless organizational genius. What more does he want? He wants a theme for a novel, he wants the secret underlying the brilliant material achievement. He is interested not in the scientific equation but in the human equation. He is not worried about survival, though it strikes us as a terribly pressing affair. He is worried about the sort of life without which it matters little whether we survive.

And now at last we arrive at a final group of novelists—the obscurer ones, the unsung, the not so widely read. Some of the novels we recognize as the finest of the 1920's were not so recognized then; *Moby Dick* in its first ten years a century ago sold fewer than 2,000 copies. Is the man whom we do not read today the one whom our wiser sons and grandsons will hail?

The very finest novels written in the past few years have dealt with the little things, the things that are not exploited in headlines. Perversely, the apparently minor aspects of our society receive the major treatment. I have mentioned some of the topics—the adolescent, the domestic scene, the regional scene, the popular activity. Our young writers do best when they ignore the spectacular highspots of our decade. They do best with the character in the humble home, in the midst of his family, the ordinary fellow holding the ordinary job.

They do best when they talk about man and woman alone, man and woman sturdy, upright, dominant, or weak, beaten, miserable, but anyway, naked man and woman, without benefit of the twentieth century—without benefit, that is, of auto, deep freeze, telephone, air-cooling, airplane, radio, television, or even one split atom: man and woman without gadgets. They do best when they write about the simple, everlasting, immortal human attributes, the pledges of affection, the handclasp, the endearment, or indeed, the jealousy and enmity.

I will not be misunderstood, I am sure, as talking of the sentimental. I mean the strong, healthy, hearty, and heartfelt emotions. I am talking about the literature that cuts back underneath our glittering plastic surfaces and reaches flesh and bone. An almost unbridgeable gulf separates what we gabble about feverishly every day upon receiving the paper, and what our writers, our consecrated, farsighted writers of potential genius, seize upon as their topics. The man in the novel is not bothered about 100 Air Force Wings; he is not being afraid of Russia; he is not losing sleep about H bomb blasts. Those matters, or the worries they awaken, are not demonstrably, freshly fundamental aspects of us as men and women. Whether they should be is another question. I am merely saying that the truth about us now in November, 1953, as the serious novelist tries to define it, lies somewhere else. The American husband, wife, son, or daughter lives the rich life, or is deprived of it, in the finest current fiction, regardless of Russia, Air Force, atoms, Kinsey, politics, peace, or war.

In other words, a new humanism begins very dimly to appear. It may be just a marking time, a literary force doomed to be displaced by something else; or it may gather strength and give shape to our next creative period. Right now there is not enough of it to justify any accurate forecast.

I hope I shall not be too embarrassed if, a quarter century hence, a novel that makes the 1950's great can be shown to have been lying at this moment on my desk. There never was a time when so many people knew so much about how to write a novel. We have more admirable talents than we can count—Calder Willingham, Lionel

Trilling, Robert Mende, Sigrid de Lima, William Styron, Carl Jonas, Robert Wernick, Alfred Hayes, Paul Bowles, Donald Wetzel, besides other names mentioned earlier.

Yet as of today great writers must be ahatching, for they are not functioning. This is a quiescent period, nothing to be ashamed of, or discouraged by, but nothing about which we should deceive ourselves, either. If from our vantage point we still cannot sight new horizons in the novel, the prospects for them have never before in our memory been so bright.

It takes only one novel to bring on the Golden Age. The husbandman customarily bemoans the fact that one rotten apple spoils the whole barrel. The critic happily foresees that one good apple makes the whole barrel.

V

NEW HORIZONS FOR POETRY

MELVILLE CANE

I have been invited, and I am deeply complimented by the invitation, to discuss a subject which as framed I am inclined to reject. The subject, "New Horizons for Poetry" comes in the form of a positive statement; it is the assumption, or at least the implication, that new horizons have been reached and won or are about to be, which I am disposed to challenge. I should be more comfortable if the subject were put in the form of a question and I shall take the liberty of changing the punctuation, and consequently the sense, to suit my own notions of where we find ourselves and where we may be going.

An horizon, figuratively speaking, connotes a range of perception and experience. More commonly it stands for the widest arc in nature accessible to our visual sense. The mind, when confronted with the idea of a new horizon is likely to picture a sea voyage where the speeding ship in its forward path constantly reveals ever new areas of space for the eye to take in. Or one may think of an Alpine climber who with each stage of his ascent beholds a vaster terrain of wonder and exaltation. Truly in so doing he leaves behind him the boundaries at the base for a seemingly limitless expanse; he enters and becomes a figure in a vaster universe. The second of these two images brings us closer to the myth of that Grecian peak where the Muses made their home.

I am not a professional literary critic but a practising poet concerned chiefly with his own problems in the art, so what I have to say here must express a purely personal point of view. And as my familiarity with the output of contemporary poets here and in England is at best incomprehensive, I shall not attempt an authoritative essay but rather, quite informally, will set down as they occur to me certain observations, certain conclusions and finally certain hopes for the poetry of tomorrow. All this, merely by way of explanation and foreword.

To add one further comment on the title, it carries for me the suggestion of a collective activity, a concerted movement. True it is that especially during the past century groups of poets have been formed and bound together by an accepted esthetic creed. To name a few of the more influential schools, there were the Parnassians, then the Symbolists, still later the Imagists, and most recently what may loosely be termed the New Metaphysicals. Each in its special way has made its contribution to the craft, and I dare say that to belong to any such coterie may offer certain psychological advantages, especially to a poet floundering, in need of reassurance, and finding such reassurance in the comforting realization that he is engaging in a common cause under the same generally recognized dogmas and goals. But to my mind such an affiliation carries the risk of hampering the activity of the imagination; a limitation unconsciously, perhaps even consciously, has been clamped on the free play of the creative process. Therefore I believe that in order to achieve the full measure of his powers a poet must transcend such theoretical confines with their imposed rigidities. We remember and read and cherish Baudelaire and Mallarmé, not so much because they headed a new movement called Symbolism, as because they employed the methods of symbolism toward a larger unrestricted fulfilment. In short, they wrote, they created as unlabeled, unticketed individuals. This was Byron's standard of judgment when in a letter to Shelley he wrote: "You know my high opinion of your poetry, because it is of no school."

What I have been trying to say is an old story, but an ever new one: it is that the great artist, regardless of his era or of the influences which may serve him, must find his sustenance and his light within himself. He must be faithful to his essence, his demon. He must follow his particular star. He must be dedicated, not dictated to. Was it not Sir Philip Sidney, who imparted that cardinal injunction: "Fool, said my muse to me, look in thy heart and write"?

Of course this does not mean that the poet should reject the past and soar on untried wings. Such would prove to be an Icarian performance even if desired. The past is always with us, and it is our business as poets to draw on it so far as it may be usable. It is our business to distinguish between what is outmoded and dead, and what is permanently alive. By means of this process of selection the salvaged past becomes the immanent present. In this operation the present parts company with the past and moves on.

This is no more than to observe the characteristic phenomena of the human mind, with its two competing pulls. Out of orthodoxy grows heterodoxy, which to the orthodox constitutes heresy. Out of convention, revolt; out of tradition, dissent. The passage from one attitude of thought to its opposite is a movement of emergence. It may represent a gain or it may not. Such progress is not necessarily an advance to a higher plane. It may be no more than a change, whether for the better or not. But the very act of emergence in itself is an act of liberation with its capacity for growth and a fresh flowering.

What, then, are the prospects?

From what influences once potent do we now turn away, finding in them diminishing vitality and value? To what sources do we look for fresh energies?

I venture the generalization that the dominant but by no means sole character of poetry in our time has been intellectual rather than emotional. The approach is conscious rather than spontaneous. The operation is calculated, and the product, by and large, is non-lyrical. Certainly, T. S. Eliot, its most influential representative, can hardly be classified as a lyric poet. In his poetry, feeling rarely mounts to passion; it is usually muted and subordinate to reflection.

The intellectual approach has been of especial value in enlarging the area of poetic interest and therefore in making available a constantly fresh body of subject matter. It is persistently exploratory; its curiosity for examining the nature of man and his place in the universe is insatiable. In this quest it takes to itself the latest discoveries of the natural sciences and becomes enriched by the revelations of psychology in penetrating the mysteries and motivations of the human soul.

And because, as I contend, this poetry originates primarily in the mind, it is not surprising that it should concern itself with wit, in the metaphysical sense, with the fashioning of conceits, and with satire and irony. For the creation of its effects it is apt to draw freely on erudition; a favorite device is to lift a line or phrase or image from an earlier author and insert it in the new poem, in order to heighten the impact of connotation. Or, it may draw from foreign tongues and literatures, as Eliot did so notably in *The Waste Land,* and as was Pound's common practise.

A question soon arises, however, concerning the amount of scholarly allusion which a poem can successfully carry. In seeking the answer one faces the ever present problem of communication. It is a commonplace, which nevertheless insists on constant reassertion, that the creative act whether in making a poem or any other form of art, is twofold, an offering and a response. The complete realization of a poem depends on the partnership between writer and reader. I am assuming a reader who is qualified by training and openmindedness to give the poet a fair hearing. The reader is both entitled and required to share in the creation by actively using his imagination. Therefore the poet cannot be satisfied with merely pleasing himself.

It seems to me that he merely pleases himself and is unfair to the reader when he operates within the thick hedge of his private scholarship. In so doing he refuses to take the reader into his confidence and creates a condition of impenetrability for which he alone is to blame. The resultant obscurity is not due to the form of statement which may well be precise and unclouded, but rather to the distance lying between the body of his material and the capacity of the reader, no matter how attentive and well meaning, to apprehend and assimilate it. A poem that requires a set of footnotes and a glossary for its elucidation has lost its esthetic virtue; it survives, if at all, as an exercise in exegetics in the guise of verse.

By the very nature of his effort to escape from past attitudes and restrictions, by the speculative consideration of his creative position, the intellectual poet is apt to become beguiled into the construction of theories and consciously or unconsciously to think as a critic rather than to feel as a poet. In examining a fair sample of modern poetry one is struck by the presence of an underlying, even dominating determination to write according to some theory, rather than out of an inner compulsion for personal utterance. Indeed it often seems as though the writer had mistaken his role and instead should have followed his true vocation as a literary critic. It is not astonishing that so many of these poets are at the same time accomplished and perceptive literary critics. But the fact that they are first of all critics and only incidentally poets is evidenced by the tone, or one might say, the tonelessness, of their verse. It lacks singularity, carries no personal mark of identification, and can be as readily assignable to one man as to another. A poem, in order to survive, must be memorable.

Turning from this sketchy inventory of the substantive matter of modern verse to the manner, the treatment, one is impressed by definite and wide gains in technique. The present day poet, regardless of esthetic school or sect is, generally speaking, and always with striking exceptions, a finer craftsman than his predecessors. His revolt from and disdain of traditional form has sharpened his appetite for experimentation and carried him far into fertile fields of innovation. In so doing he has been aided and influenced by many movements already current, such as imagism, the process of free association, and the introduction of straight prose into the corpus of his compositions. And, of course, free verse.

His debt to imagism is deep and abiding, for it was the Imagists in the earlier decades of the century who stressed the need of a closer scrutiny of the natural world in order to extract and set down the full and exact flavor and color of each object. The modern poet has thus been made increasingly and more subtly aware of his sensorial equipment and of his need to avoid vagueness and imprecision.

Along with his concern for accuracy the poet of our time constantly strives for wider extensions and expansions of his craftsmanship and his subject matter. He opens up the channel of his unconscious and lets flow its unpredictable stream, to wander however waywardly it may. He surrenders to the mysterious surrealistic life of dream, with its rich yield of hidden symbols. In the operation his art develops intricacy, complexity, a more flexible texture and an undercurrent of counterpoint. Musically speaking, the modern poet works for harmony rather than for melody.

As to meter, the very nature of the modern poet's enterprise seems to call for free verse and the subordination of rhyme. Paradoxically, free verse to be successfully employed must obey its own laws of form and design. Its freedom is not absolute but comparative. In the hands of its most competent users one always senses the presence of an underlying control. Pegasus is still directed in his flights, but with a looser rein.

A modern poem, technically, may not unlikely turn out to be a composite creation, a mosaic with a free verse base, lines of disparate lengths and stresses, lines that match equally, beat for beat and end in pure rhyme, and possibly with a return for the moment to the meter of blank verse, the traditional iambic pentameter. To ingredients such as these the poet may add for more cunning effects the devices of sprung rhythm, employed by Gerard Manley Hopkins, assonance, and, perhaps most importantly, a mixture of straight prose. Let it be noted in passing, however, that the skillful composer of *avant garde* verse is equally at home in the traditional meters. The English poet, William Empson, for example, has taken the villanelle, an artificial French form of strictest pattern, and endowed it with vitality.

The introduction of prose into the texture presents a question of legitimacy. As a means of creating contrast it doubtless has value, but by and large it would seem to constitute an alien medium inimical to the laws and spirit of versemaking. However, in the adroit hands of a Robert Frost, what was nothing more than ordinary prose in its inception can be transmuted and raised to the estate of poetry. The danger in the use of prose lies in its tendency to become overdiscursive and conversational, in short, to be more prose than poetry. Too many poets are talkers when they ought to be singers.

Modern poetry continues in the line of Wordsworth and Browning and Hardy to annex outlying territories of living speech; it does not hesitate to employ current idioms, contemporary slang, the daily vocabulary of the marketplace. "Poetic language" no longer exists in any aristocratic sense; all language, democratically, is qualified to serve, the only stricture being that of fitness to the theme and the mood.

The advances made over the poetry of the nineteenth century would seem to relate principally to matters of technique and attitude rather than of imagination and vision. The nineteenth century poet, especially in America, was generally content to work in the established meters and forms; until the advent of Poe and Sidney Lanier there is little evidence of that kind of esthetic curiosity and inquiry we find among the moderns. By omitting Whitman from this category I know I am taking an unpopular stand. I contend, however, that while Whitman proved a mighty force in liberating our poetry from the shackles of convention, his motivation and ideals seem essentially those of a religious and humanitarian crusader. His disposition and talents were primarily those of the orator, the preacher, and the prophet. We gladly and gratefully acknowledge our debt to him for his majestic biblical line and as the founder and father of free verse, but we should not overlook the fact that as artist *per se* he was lacking in the necessary responsibility. Except for a few sublimely glorious successes his torrential poetic energy, one must admit, rushes unharnessed and headlong.

Whitman's influence on modern poetry, whether intellectual or lyrical has been undeniably farreaching and of solid worth. But has it always been a good influence? Can it not be fairly asserted that the scriptural rhythms of the King James version of the Bible, however noble, are essentially those of prose lifted to its most exalted level? And is it not a cardinal fault in modern verse that its tendency to sacrifice and scrap the basic distinctions between verse and prose has often worked an injury to poetry? Has it not watered poetry down?

In our estimate of the many technical gains of the poetry of our generation we must properly take into account its weaknesses; the most serious, as it seems to me, has been the failure to recognize that in his legitimate roving along new and wider avenues of expression, in his pursuit of flexibility and firmness of outline, the modern poet has often let these preoccupations run away with him, to the loss of his essential purity and his animating flame.

Stephen Spender states well the difficulty.

Students might be puzzled to answer the question why it is that so frequently a sophisticated critic, with his grasp of the complexities that naturally condition poetry is not able to write poems better than those of the comparatively simple-minded poets. The answer may be that the shock of art is lost when it is absorbed into a complicated machinery of exegesis.[1]

That the constant pursuit of finer spun complexities and textures has led many a modern poet into the labyrinth of obscurity is a fact apparent to all who attempt to penetrate the mysteries. One wonders whether a dead end has not been reached; whether to quote George Barker, another British poet, we have not had our fill of "that exhaustive nagging after effect that has come to be called metaphysical writing"; whether one cannot have too much of a good thing, and whether the thing was ever as good as it seemed on first impression.

Observations such as these are signs, or at least hints that we may be witnessing the decline and demise of the intellectualistic regime and that it may be superseded by the election to office of the "comparatively simpleminded" opposition. We might borrow "it's time for a change" as a campaign slogan, not because change in itself is desirable, but because any administration too long in power inevitably generates seeds of decay. In the present instance it would seem that the original ardors are cooling off, that the original springs of inspiration are becoming choked under the pressures of formalism, cultism, even intellectual snobbism. Overdeep interest in the way a thing is done rather than in the thing itself, overemphasis on form to the slight of substance—these are the invariable omens of decadence in any art, let alone the poetic.

The art of the intellectual poets was never a popular art; it made its appeal to a sophisticated elite, and the more deeply inbred it became, the farther it removed itself from the natural longings and needs of the human heart. Yet it was Ezra Pound who wisely announced in the springtime of his career that one of the first purposes of writing is "to make glad the heart of man." It does not lie within the province of this paper to show how far short Pound fell in his fidelity to this purpose or how his involvement in new skills and alien creeds poisoned, to paraphrase Herbert Read, both his heart and his verses.

[1] Stephen Spender, "The New Orthodoxies," *New Republic*, Vol. 128, #30, July 27, 1953, p. 16.

The ironic comment on life, so congenial to the intellectual temperament and so effectively presented in much of modern verse, is liable if carried too far to lead to a condition of cynicism and a sense of futility. In contemplating the lot of man and his struggle for spiritual survival and perfectability the poet runs the risk of emphasizing his weaknesses at the expense of the nobility of his aspirations, his faith and his hope. This myopic distortion creates a false picture, in fact a base and disheartening caricature, for it leaves out the essential characteristics of man; it ignores his nature as a moral, idealistic creature.

While preparing these random notes I had the good luck to come upon a novel rich in worldly wisdom, and written from a point of view in many ways corresponding with my own reactions to the current state of poetry. It is entitled *Zorba the Greek;* its author is Nikos Kazantzakēs. The story is told in the first person; the narrator is an overcultivated philosopher and man of letters, subjectively imprisoned in his ivory tower, sick at heart and desperate to come to terms with life, and to experience and partake of its riches. In the course of his turmoil he turns to a volume of so-called "pure" poetry which had entranced him as a young man. But now, in his maturity the spell is broken. This is how he sets down his disillusionment: "I closed the book, opened it again, and finally threw it down. For the first time in my life it all seemed bloodless, odorless, void of any human substance. Pale-blue, hollow words in a vacuum. Perfectly distilled water without any bacteria, but also without any nutritive substances. Without life. . . . The ardent aspirations of the heart, laden with earth and seed, had become a flawless intellectual game, a clever aerial and intricate architecture. . . . All these things which had formerly so fascinated me appeared this morning to be no more than cerebral acrobatics and refined charlatanism." [2]

How faithfully, how percipiently, Kazantzakēs presents our present esthetic dilemma! It is from this realization of aridity and emptiness that the heart and the mind instinctively and protectively recoil, to seek elsewhere for nourishment and light. The soul, to use a word in partial eclipse, requires the energizing sustenance of affirmation, or else it perishes.

[2] Nikos Kazantzakēs, *Zorba the Greek,* J. Lehmann, London, 1952, pp. 141–142.

I have attempted, however superficially, fragmentarily and dogmatically, to discuss certain aspects and attitudes of contemporary poetry that have impressed me in one way or another. I have dwelt almost exclusively on the position of the intellectuals, as it undoubtedly has exercised the most compulsive influence on the character of the verse of the period, both as to substance and craftsmanship. I have tried to show in what respects it has usefully advanced the art and successfully pioneered into regions heretofore unexplored. Similarly, I have endeavored to point out the inevitable infirmities and false turnings implicit in an adventure so earnestly and courageously undertaken. And, finally, I now come to consider the source of our dissatisfactions as the movement loses its early appeal and momentum. What the intellectual poets seem either to have overlooked or deliberately rejected is the fundamental indispensable conception that poetry is song, the outpouring of the heart under the stress of feeling. It issues forth spontaneously, impulsively, passionately, defiant of rational interference or restraint. It arises out of a state of innocence and wonder; it flows with intuitive vigor and confidence to reveal and report the innermost truth, the mysterious essence.

This great gift of song the intellectuals, preoccupied with systems of prosody and with calculated thought, have seen fit to renounce as something possibly too emotional, or too romantic, or, even too sentimental. Whatever their motive in this regard they have served poetry ill. The task of oncoming poets is plain: they must rescue their art from sterility. To do so they must first of all recover the lost quality of innocence, they must follow their intuitions wheresoever they may lead and not be afraid of ecstasy; they must recapture spontaneity and music and magic and the capacity for unhampered flight; they must dedicate themselves to Dionysus, the untamed god.

Out of such endeavors as these one can hope, if not for a new horizon, at least for a resurgence of health. I am advocating not merely the return to lyricism, important though that may be, but more comprehensively for a corrective to the direction modern poetry has taken, and for a saner outlook on man's place in the universe, his uncynical adjustment to this age of anxiety, and his renewal of faith in his personal destiny.

Technically speaking, I have the feeling that the new poets, while sensibly taking advantage of the nuances and subtleties of modern verse, will tend to reexamine the traditional meters and forms and refresh them with sharper awareness of their possibilities.

I cannot foresee at this moment [October, 1953] the formation of any new school or cult, and should regard any such eventuality as unfortunate. The art of poetry is not a collective product concocted from a common recipe, but is made up of the diverse contributions of dissimilar individuals, each according to his fashion.

What I presently observe is far from being a wasteland, but rather a soil in need of refertilization. I find encouraging evidence of fruitfulness among young poets in both England and the United States, and I am especially impressed with the appearance on the scene of two figures of significant stature, the Welsh poet, Dylan Thomas, and the English playwright, Christopher Fry. What makes them particularly welcome and attractive is a pervasive joyousness, gusto, and exuberance, and in the case of Fry, a Shakespearean warmth of comedy. They sing because singing delights them. They sing, as true poets must always sing, of the eternal themes of love and death and natural beauty and man's battle with destiny in the face of heavy odds. They create out of fullness and strength and spiritual health. Thomas, so tragically cut off in the prime of his powers, lives on both in accomplishment and as a future influence.

It takes no gift of prophecy to report that the tide is turning.

VI

NEW MOVEMENTS IN RECENT LITERATURE

BY

OSCAR J. CAMPBELL

A few weeks ago my eye was startled by an advertisement in a New York paper. It described a movie of Mickey Spillane in the following alluring terms: "Rough, raw, brutal, and sexy." Just because this author, widely read, I am told, by the younger generation, is a crude artist, the words "rough, raw, brutal, and sexy," describe in their nakedness some of the most popular and most influential movements in recent literature. Although we shall rise at once from Spillane's artistic level, we shall see that at least one of the adjectives in the advertisement could serve as an appropriate description of almost every one of the works I plan to discuss.

None of the distinctive features of most of the new literary works would have come into vogue if their authors had not consciously cut themselves off from the past. Religious, moral, and philosophical conceptions sanctified by time and tested by generations of human experience are contemptuously rejected by the leading practitioners of the new literary modes. André Gide makes this rejection preliminary to the problems he treats in his novels. He believes that a person's moral and intellectual heritage, his family, the experiences of childhood and youth, and the habits and principles derived therefrom unite to impose on an individual a mechanical and factitious self. Therefore, the only way to bring the true self to the surface is to discard almost everything inherited and everything acquired up to the moment of the liberation of the inner self from the paralyzing weight of tradition and custom. From this declaration comes his theory that the novel should deal, not with society, but with some unresolved personal

73

psychological difficulty—some debate between a man's conscience and his subconscious.

Joseph Wood Krutch in his recent volume, *Modernism in Modern Drama,* makes clear Ibsen's responsibility for the launching of this ethical revolution. For example, in *Ghosts* the dramatist shows not merely that inherited disease haunts successive generations but also that the ghosts of all sorts of dead ideas paralyze and frustrate living men and women, for, as Ibsen makes clear in his later plays, all truth and all moral imperatives are relative to the temper of the age. Rebecca West, the new woman in *Rosmersholm,* has given up all of the articles of faith belonging to what she would call "the myth of Christianity" and has renounced its entire ethical system, as well. The general effect of this and most of Ibsen's later plays is to record the total disintegration of the ethical and spiritual Christian cosmos and to preach the need of a transvaluation of values. These are the negative aspects of his work. Ibsen was primarily a great destroyer. He did not establish a new system of moral values. That task he left to Nietzsche.

However, Ibsen did start literature upon a fruitful course of development. He more and more turned his interest to tensions created by unresolved conflicts in the minds of his characters. Like the two principals in George Meredith's *Modern Love,* his men and women are destroyed by what is false within. Hedda Gabler resembles other characters in Ibsen's later works in becoming a case history for a book of abnormal psychology. Hence the play may be regarded as the first in a long line of works of fiction dealing with neurotic characters. That is a second movement in recent literature, which, though its roots may thrust far back of the immediate present, is, in some of its recent manifestations, an altogether new development.

Other literary forces soon united with the growing interest in psychologically abnormal characters, with the result that the trend was both strengthened and modified. Zola's particular form of determinism, which he called naturalism, enriched the value of the dramatic technique developed by Ibsen. If man, as Zola contended, was the creature of his heredity and his environment, he could be shown to be the prisoner of the personality bequeathed him by his forebears and shaped by the world in which he had his being. As the formative influence of a wretched social milieu is easier to show than that of a healthy and pleasant one, writers drew more and more desperately realistic pictures of social and moral degradation. It is through the door of naturalism as a philosophy and an artistic method that brutality and violence entered literature. They formed a new sort of primitivism to serve as the milieu for neurotic characters. From this union comes the uncensored horrors of *From Here to Eternity* and the raw power of many of John Steinbeck's novels. In his most recent *East of Eden,* for example, he has created in Cathy a typical heroine of the new romanticism. She is a monster of evil. There is no sin of which she is not guilty: murder, arson, adultery, and other sexual vagaries so horrible that Steinbeck dared only to hint at them. She becomes a financially successful proprietor of a house of prostitution where she provides her patrons with all sorts of forbidden and outré sexual indulgence. Steinbeck tells this story of violence and of crime heaped upon crime with all the power and literary skill of which he is capable. Yet in essence *East of Eden* appeals to no higher moral impulses than Mickey Spillane's crude cinema. Both are equally rough, raw, brutal, and sexy. Both are products of the cult of violence which has become one of the most vigorous movements in recent literature.

The first and simplest result of the importance attributed to the private mind of the individual was the invention of the technique known as the stream of consciousness. This was delicately and charmingly employed in the novels of Virginia Woolf, borrowed by James Joyce for the obscene reverie of Mrs. Bloom in *Ulysses,* and developed into a method of dramatic construction by Eugene O'Neill in his *Strange Interlude.*

This technique was given the dignity of an artistic theory by the doctrines of expressionism, of which the philosophy and methods were invented by a group of modern painters and only later applied to literature. They appear principally in the drama, most notably in the plays of August Strindberg. Like the stream of consciousness in literature, expressionism also exalts the importance of the subconscious mind of the individual. The essence of its theory and practise is that the most significant material for the artist is composed of objects as apprehended by a mind when possessed by some strong emotion. The feeling of a conventional artist was normal enough to meet yours and mine on natural phenomena, objectively observed. Cows ruminating in a calm landscape or a tree lashed by the wind did the trick. But the ego of the expressionistic artist, complicated by disordered emanations from the subconscious is too particular, and his emotions too private and atypical, to be communicated by such ordinary means. So he distorts reality to communicate the look of a tree or of a human face, when his ego is distorted by a complex of undigested emotions.

When the observing ego is that of a neurotic, the result is a surrealistic work of art, such as Joyce's *Finnegans Wake*. The apparently chaotic disorder of the materials of that work is a projection of the disorder and complexity of the unrestrained and undirected stream of forgotten experience rising from Joyce's subconscious mind and stirred into a kind of witches' broth by the pranks of a mad cook in that subterranean kitchen. As Joyce's mind was richly stored, commentators on his text find it a fascinating intellectual exercise to unravel the strands of meaning and association twisted beyond recognition in the inchoate, often superficially meaningless mass of words. The charm of this exercise encourages the members of the cult of unintelligibility to outdo themselves in obscurity. Joyce undoubtedly believed that *Finnegans Wake* was a derisively concocted symbol of the confusion and intellectual nihilism of modern civilization. But by continuously underscoring the importance of completely subjective experiences he has progressively disintegrated the form of the modern novel.

From this technique of the raw stream of consciousness, it was an easy and inevitable step to the technique of the dream. Strindberg took the lead in this development in his trilogy, *To Damascus,* and then *The Dream Play*. Most important for the dreamer is his emancipation from the tyranny of both time and space. And against that timeless background the mind weaves strange patterns, a medley of memories and free associations, all of them escapes from reality, for the only reality in these plays is the mind of the dreamer and its phantasmagoria. The reality of the characters is also insubstantial, subject to constant changes in outline, even in identity. These constructions of

Strindberg's dream plays are on the whole painful and tormenting. But from this miasma of mind rises an atmosphere of pity for the lot of wretched human beings.

The latest play to show the influence of Strindberg's dream technique is Tennessee Williams's *Camino Real.* This drama greatly confused the critics because few of them had the faintest idea of what the playwright was about. It was like Strindberg's plays, set outside time and place: for Lord Byron, who escapes to die for an ideal in Greece, is here, so is a haggard, crumpled Casanova, a Camille who is reduced to buying love, and a Don Quixote who escapes into the happy world of his own illusions. But with these figures of the past appears an American prizefighter with a bad heart, a cooch dancer, officers of a Gestapo who beat up the poor common creatures of the streets, and street cleaners who cart off dead bodies to a garbage dump. All the action takes place in a square in a city vaguely placed somewhere in Latin America. On one side of this square is a hotel whose proprietor is full of haughty contempt for all who come into his view. On the other side is a flop house, a pawnshop, and a house of prostitution. This amply inhabited space is cut off from the rest of the world by interminable deserts and unpassable mountains, and is surrounded by a high wall. It is designed as a symbol of the trap in which mankind has been caught, or of the sink into which all its representatives have drained. The technique is like that of a dream. The play is indeed the nightmare of a man who has looked with aversion upon the world in which he, with the rest of us, must live.

Into this complex of literary movements came the psychiatry of Sigmund Freud, in which the subconscious or id, as he called it, assumed unprecedented importance. This id is the storehouse of all man's primitive impulses boiling there in a completely barbaric state. When they escape into the conscious mind there begins a struggle with the superego for the control of the ego. Because the id is the source of drives to artistic creation, many mistakenly believe that they are the pure stuff of art and literature, that any control or direction given them by reason only weakens and perverts them.

Sexual drives also originate in the id in all their pristine rawness. Because Freud attributes great importance to these drives in the growth and stabilization of personality and transcendent importance in the fashioning of neurotics, modern literature is obsessed with sex. It is not unnatural therefore that sex has taken the place in literature that used to be occupied by love. Most modern writers seem to think they are the same thing, Kinsey, for example.

In many of his works André Gide exhorts us, crying, "Liberate the id. That is your true self. If you fail to do so, you are in for trouble." Michel, the principal figure in Gide's *L'immoraliste* is really a homosexual, but convention forbids him to liberate that kind of buried self. He tries to do so by ruthlessly eliminating from his nature everything acquired and by indulging in everything forbidden by custom. On his estate he is fascinated by the most primitive and brutal of his farmhands. He catches a boy, Alcide, poaching and joins him in poaching on his own estate. In his travels he associates with vile sailors and foul tramps even while his wife is dying. The tension in his nature is between discipline and convention, on the one hand, and anarchy and wanton destruction on the other. The story is not specifically about homosexuality, but of the effects of any sort of suppression of a man's real nature. It makes him a rebel who is irresistibly attracted to everything that his conscience forbids his id and is unable to adjust the conflict between the two parts of his mind. The novel is Gide's proof that if an individual's most fundamental impulses are stifled, they will break out in violent anti-social conduct. The novel also exhibits two movements in recent literature: the first, a tendency to emancipate the self from all social and moral restraint; the second, a movement toward the primitive drives in a man's nature. This anti-social bias of many modern authors has tended to make them self-condemned pariahs, outcasts from the communal life of their time, and to drive them to adopt a harsh moral iconoclasm.

Another widespread movement in modern and recent literature is the impulse to translate every idea, every aspiration, every criticism of life into metaphorical language, or, to put it in another way, to see everything in the emotional light of a metaphor. One of the most vivid and prolonged employments of this method appears in Franz Kafka's *Metamorphosis*. The title is ironic, inviting comparison with Ovid's romantic legends of transformation. In fact, the short novel is nothing but the statement and development of one figure. The story is that of a poor creature who awakens one morning to find that during the night he has been turned into a huge insect, a mammoth cockroach. It is his disgust and his agony during his efforts to get out of the room into which his family has naturally locked him and to communicate with what he had supposed was his own flesh and blood, that forms the plot of the tale.

It is Kafka's symbolic method of conveying to his readers the desperate feelings of a man who imagines he has been rejected by those nearest and dearest to him, that everyone regards him with a mixture of aversion and disgust. The symbolic method in this case is strikingly successful. A conventional narrative could have produced a comparable human situation and a comparable emotion only through a story of much greater length and of much more intellectual intricacy—a story only the greatest of novelists could have been capable of writing.

In *The Trial* Kafka presents through the leisurely expansion of a trope modern man's sense of confusion and frustration as he blindly moves through life. Although superficially the work develops in the manner of a conventional novel, its essential meaning is not on the surface. The plot concerns a man who is arrested for he knows not what, is submitted to successive, chimerical examinations by the police and to fantastic trials in grotesquely organized courts of law. Finally he is taken to a quarry, where two executioners, after ridiculously courteous formalities, lay his head upon a boulder, produce knives from the inner pockets of their frock coats, and offer to let him stab himself to death. When he refuses, one of his captors chokes him while the other plunges a knife into his heart and turns it around twice. Just before his end the victim sees in a window far above this desert of stones a faint, insubstantial figure, who stretches his arms out toward him in a futile gesture of sympathy and aid.

The novel is a morality play or a pilgrim's progress in reverse. Its immediate relevance was to human life in Nazi Germany, but it is also an allegory of the typical human pilgrimage in the modern world. The pilgrim is thrust into a mysteriously malign universe, pursued by incomprehensively hostile forces which finally destroy him with stony cruelty. The only sympathy and understanding available to him comes from on high, but it is vague, remote, and futile. This creature looking down in belated and unserviceable sympathy on the man destroyed by the hard, dark modern world is all the help and comfort that God can now give to desperately beset modern man. These works of Kafka, may not be recent, but they represent in striking form the primary importance of the symbol and metaphor in contemporary literature.

Thomas Mann, whom many critics regard as the greatest of recent novelists, has always emphasized the symbolical aspects of his fiction. His last work, *Dr. Faustus,* has all the characteristics of a morality, but, like so many pieces of contemporary literature, it turns a conventional form upside down. It is a symbolic description of the political and moral ruin of modern Germany. The protagonist, Adrian Leverkuehn, is both Faust and Germany and in particular Nazi Germany. Adrian is a composer. Mann, who loved music but feared its hypnotic power, believed that Germany's devotion to music had seduced her from reality and sound bourgeois morality. Music to Mann leads its devotees to moral death. So Adrian in being a composer is Mephistopheles, as well as Faust. Adrian, like Nietzsche, deliberately contracts a venereal disease, because he believes a mind so afflicted will produce a more original and more compelling beauty. In the grandiose striving of Adrian's later work, Mann suggests both the supposedly diseased Beethoven of the late sonatas and quartets, Gustav Mahler, and Hugo Wolf, who also ended his life in madness. Mann clearly expects his readers to see in Adrian's breakdown a symbolic picture of "the death agonies of the Third Reich." And in the multiplicity of the analogies which the reader must himself discover Mann is saying, "To be a German, is like Faust to be damned in this world if not in the next." The novel, with its complicated, rich structure, with its brilliantly conceived and intricately developed parallels to many modern musicians, to many political events, to Faustus, and to Germany, is perhaps the one work in recent literature with a symbolic structure which shows positive genius.[1]

[1] In this analysis of *Dr. Faustus,* I am greatly indebted to Henry Hatfield, *Thomas Mann,* New Directions Books, Norfolk, Connecticut, 1951.

In poetry the contemporary obsession with symbol takes a more general, if more unintelligible form. The preferred technique of modern poetry is supposed to owe much to a prophetic essay of T. E. Hulme, entitled "Romanticism and Classicism." He expressed there a belief that literature was on the verge of a new classical movement. That it was going to become accurate, precise, and definite. That in poetry these virtues could be attained only by the abandonment of faded romantic metaphors in favor of new ones which would shed the kind of light needed to illuminate the new emotions which should be the concern of the new poetry.

T. S. Eliot is the fulfilment of Hulme's prophecy. It was the new symbols in his early poetry which startled and waylaid his readers. Most of them are now stale from repetition in the prose of criticism. "I have measured out my life with coffee and spoons"; "evening is spread out against the sky like a patient etherized upon a table"; "Spit out the butt ends of my days and ways"; "I have seen the eternal Footman hold my coat and snicker." These figures betray Eliot's admiration for Donne and other seventeenth century metaphysical poets. Metaphors of this sort appear most abundantly in the poems written in his *The Waste Land* period and that immediately preceding it. The poems strike first at the abuses and confusions of his world, and later at its rootlessness and its aimlessness. Even primitive people, in Eliot's view, were closer than we to the eternal virtues, for they were eternally conscious of the powers of life and death, as their fertility rites and their folklore bear witness. Orientals, too, with their highly developed art of contemplation, are less the prisoners of futility. The truth is that Western civilization suffers from a killing, spiritual drought. It has thus become a wasteland. To be sure, Eliot later sought to dissociate his own point of view from that expressed in the poem, saying that it showed certain people their illusion of disillusionment.

The sense of confusion and inconsequence which the work creates is heightened by Eliot's rhetorical manner, the abrupt transition from image to image, his application of the constructive principles of a fugue, his arrangement of verbal patterns enhanced, the effects at which he aimed. *The Waste Land* theme was popular in the 1920's and the poem was often imitated. The artistic method which Eliot employed in its development, along with his use of free verse, is still the preferred speech of many contemporary poets.

Eliot's spirit did not continue to dwell in the Waste Land. He found an escape and a refuge in orthodox Christianity, as *Ash Wednesday* shows. It is a poem of Christian humility as the lines

> Teach us to care and not to care
> Teach us to sit still [2]

clearly prove. On Ash Wednesday Eliot gives up both hope and despair in the face of death. The poem is a declaration and application of his literal faith in Christianity which non-believers may translate into imaginative faith if they can. But for both kinds of audience the work is a little masterpiece. *Murder in the Cathedral* presents Eliot's central conviction in dramatic form. In dramatizing Becket's death, he develops the same theme of submission to God. True martyrdom to Becket is not so much the sacrifice of his life as the submission of his will to the Divine will.

One of the reasons that Eliot's influence has not been more extensive is that he finds it difficult to translate his ideas of salvation into terms of contemporary life. That is to me the fatal weakness of *The Cocktail Party.* The most important theme in the play is the story of Celia Coplestone's salvation through a martyrdom more appropriate for the legend of a medieval saint than for a woman who measures out her life with cocktail glasses. She goes to Kinkanja to nurse African natives dying of a pestilence. During an insurrection of the natives she is captured and crucified near an anthill, from which we are given to understand insects swarmed to devour her body, even before she had died. If Eliot had only invented a method of salvation available to sinners in our world, the play would have been better and its influence wider.

But Eliot persists in his belief that escape from the Waste Land must come by way of some phase of medieval Christianity. In his *Four Quartets,* difficult poems because of the poet's lavish employ-

[2] T. S. Eliot, *Collected Poems, 1909–1935,* Harcourt, Brace & Company, New York, 1936, p. 110.

ment of metaphor, Eliot says that man must find his personal salvation in Christian meditation as prolonged and devoted as that practised in ancient Oriental cults. The first of the four elegies begins as follows:

> Time present and time past
> Are both perhaps present in time future,
> And time future contained in time past[3]

Man's spirit, says Eliot, like all fundamental events of religion and of life itself, exists out of time. And he shows in multifarious ways how we can escape from selfish emotion, from all effort, into a rose garden where existence has the permanent intensity of prayer.

In this poem, as R. P. Blackmur says, Eliot's mind is filled by "an onion of metaphors" which he peels off in successive lines. This is an apt description of the method of composition employed by the most highly regarded of recent poets. They use metaphor as did the seventeenth century metaphysicians and produce a thoroughly baroque piece of art. This is the method of the late lamented Dylan Thomas, widely heralded as the greatest lyric poet of the contemporary world, a modern Keats, as the following poem shows.

> When all my five and country senses see,
> The fingers will forget green thumbs and mark
> How, through the halfmoon's vegetable eye,
> Husk of young stars and handfull zodiac,
> Love in the frost is pared and wintered by,
> The whispering ears will watch love drummed away
> Down breeze and shell to a discordant beach,
> And, lashed to syllables, the lynx tongue cry
> That her fond wounds are mended bitterly.
> My nostrils see her breath burn like a bush.
> My one and noble heart has witnesses
> In all love's countries, that will grope awake;
> And when blind sleep drops on the spying senses,
> The heart is sensual, though five eyes break.[4]

[3] T. S. Eliot, *Four Quartets,* Harcourt, Brace & Company, New York, 1943, p. 3.
[4] Dylan Thomas, *Collected Poems,* New Directions, New York, 1953, p. 90.

All of the avenues of escape from the Waste Land which Eliot explored have been followed by others sometimes further and with less sensitivity. His early admiration of primitive culture was developed by D. H. Lawrence, for one, in a manner which Eliot would hardly have approved.

In *The Plumed Serpent,* for example, Lawrence draws a picture of an ancient Mexican community of men and women who think not with their brains but with their bodies, acting as though the body were "the flame of the soul." Utterly natural men and women like these, so Lawrence suggests, are capable of uniting, not for the acquisition of power but for the dissemination of tenderness. Such communities, he insists, would recreate the world by eradicating all the evil passions of greed and force which have made a shambles of the modern life. This is another manifestation of that creed of primitivism which flows like a violently red river through the parched landscape of modern literature.

Eliot's doctrine of escape from time in order to devote one's self to prayerlike meditation has been made the stuff of fiction by Aldous Huxley in his latest novels. *After Many a Summer Dies the Swan* is superficially a story of jealousy, lust, and murder in a castle where an old gentleman named Stoyte, whose resemblance to Hearst is too close to be coincidental, has established his beautiful mistress. But the meaning of the action is suggested by the comments of Mr. Propter. There are, according to him, three levels of life. First is the animal level, where good exists as the proper functioning of the organism in accordance with the laws of its own being. Then there is the human level where men destroy what they build, destroy it even while they build, for they build with elements of destruction fashioned by two evil forces, time and personal craving of every sort. On the highest level, that of eternity, good exists in a form of knowledge of the world without desire or aversion. Before the end of the volume we see that Mr. Propter's philosophy is a form of Yoga. For the peace which comes to one on the level of eternity springs from the knowledge that individual souls are an illusion, and whatever they create insane, but that all separate beings are potentially united in eternity. One incident in the novel will show how this philosophy becomes a principle of its construction. Poor Pete, an idealistic youth, and Propter's eager disciple, having for the first time felt the exaltation of living on this highest level, takes an elevator to the top of the castle that he may look out over the loveliness of the mountain as the sun sinks and feel the peace of God. But instead he sees Virginia, the old man's mistress, lying on the couch in great spiritual distress caused by her treatment by the man of pure evil, Dr. Obispo. As Pete begins to stroke the girl's hair as though imploring her to be happy, he is shot to death by the old Stoyte, who mistakes him for Dr. Obispo. There could be no more melodramatic way for Huxley to show the folly and danger of descending from the level of eternity to the middle level of evil human living.

My picture of new and not so new movements in recent literature has been a dark one. It is true that books besides those I have discussed are being written and widely read. But those I have used to illustrate the important tendencies in contemporary literature are the influential volumes. They are the ones read and admired by the youth of today. It is well that a gathering such as this should face this disturbing fact. That it should be aware of the withdrawal of much contemporary literature from the concerns of the common man and of the man of common sense; that it should note with concern its addiction to violence, its exploitation of sex, and, in general, its spiritual poverty. It should realize, too, that the correctives offered in literature: the return to all the doctrines and practises of medieval Christianity: the withdrawal from active life, from personality itself, and a flight to a haven where one can find timeless peace in non-personal experience, that none of these religious and pseudo-religious counterpoises to moral nihilism, appeal to young men and women of the modern world. Only by facing these ominous facts can men of spiritual goodwill intelligently gird themselves for the battle which must be fought for the soul of the Western world.

VII

NEW HORIZONS IN MUSIC

BY

HENRY D. COWELL

A distinction must be made between new musical horizons themselves and the ability of interested auditors to appreciate them. There
have been many new philosophies and materials in all of the arts;
these pop up every once in a while. It is almost inevitable that they
are at first not understood, that they are later understood by a small
group, and still later find general acceptance.

Music is no exception to this type of unfoldment, but the process
is slower than in other arts because literacy in music is extremely
rare; so rare, in fact, that most people do not even know in what it
consists. In reading, one thinks the sound of the word one sees.
Literacy in music consists of hearing in one's mind the sounds of
notes as written. Although this end can in a great majority of cases
be accomplished by training (even with people who consider themselves unmusical), general training of laymen usually does not include the subject at all, and even many professional performers have
never gained the ability to do more than to locate written sounds in
their voices or on their instruments. So literacy, for the most part, is
current only among a few composers and conductors. Musicologists
deal in words concerning music, and are usually not much interested
in the actual sounds of which they write.

A painting or a piece of sculpture may be looked at as long as there
is interest, and reproductions of old and new things may be examined
at length. Literature may be read and reread. Even in the case of a
play, while one does not obtain a full concept without seeing it
staged, a very good idea of it may nevertheless be formed through

87

reading the text. The dance is in between—some ideas may be had from looking at still pictures, but for the most part one must see the movement to appreciate it.

Most auditors know music only as they hear it unfold; once sounded the tones disappear, and their relationships tend to be forgotten. Even on several hearings, only a few snatches of tune and a bit of rhythm are apt to be remembered; and most values in new music are more complex.

Before new music became so much more available in recorded form, opportunities to hear important new works were astonishingly few. Obviously for new music to assume meaning for general auditors, it must be heard frequently; and although recordings and radio broadcasts of recordings have speeded up the process, performances are still too few to enable a rapid advance of comprehension of new musical values. Music itself has kept pace with modern literature, architecture, and pictorial arts; public acceptance has lagged.

The first third of this century saw a great many innovations in musical materials. Some music abandoned the idea of a key, or tonal center; some music employed several tonal centers simultaneously. Irregular and constantly changing rhythms appeared, often several at the same time. Chords were built on seconds and fourths, as well as the traditional thirds, and combinations of tones which would have been classified as discords previously were used more and more extensively, and freed of the necessity for resolution. Counterpoint was applied to dissonance as well as consonance, and instead of confining itself to seven tone major and minor scales, used all twelve tones in the Western musical system to roam about in with entire freedom. Thus in the teen years and the twenties many new tonal and rhythmic horizons were discovered. To many listeners, these horizons are still in the process of being discovered, and the term, "modern music," is used to describe the experimental works written during that period. Actually, however, barriers were reached in this sort of experiment in the mid-twenties. Our musical system possesses but twelve tones. Every scale that can be formed within this system is set down and may be found in Nicolas Slonimsky's *Thesaurus of Scales and Melodic Patterns. The Schillinger System of Musical*

Composition shows how to form every possible chord, and all rhythmic combinations far beyond any in actual use. The "twelve tone row" system of counterpoint as taught by Arnold Schoenberg insists on the use of every tone in the musical system in every melody and in all harmonic patterns. By the early thirties this system had been thoroughly explored. This overlapped a change of direction in new horizons which began in the twenties, when Stravinsky, who had been noted for extreme experiment in dissonance and rhythm, turned "neo-classical." The swarm of young followers who had cheered each new discord and syncopation in Stravinsky's earlier works were at first completely baffled by this new turn, and for the most part did not like or understand it. It is, indeed, easy to be fooled by the deceptive apparent simplicity. Most sympathetic listeners, one fears, listen as classicists, and enjoy the result because it sounds like music they know, usually with a few odd spots which can be glossed over or forgotten, even though they may be momentarily disturbing. But this is not the way one is expected to listen. Neo-classical music is designed to contain all the experience of the experimental horizons; it is a return to older models following such experience. To listen to this music properly, not only the composer but the hearer must have lived through the era of complex tonal and rhythmic relations, and recognize the implications of these relationships in the studied and stylized neo-simplicity. Only after reaching and to some extent understanding the horizon at the barriers of the experimental era is one prepared to move toward the horizon of the neo-classical. The approach is made no easier by the fact that many listeners do not recognize that this *is* a new and difficult horizon, and believe that they understand the results through a simple, direct approach. Stravinsky and Prokofiev have both been pioneers in neo-classicism, with many followers in France, and through the famous teacher, Nadia Boulanger, in America among composers of the "Boston School." It would be hard to find any successful composer since the beginning of the forties, whether he be radical or conservative, in the popular or serious field, and no matter from what country, who has not been influenced by both the experimental and neo-classic eras.

There are still some vestiges of investigation in the two fields so far mentioned. All possible rhythms have not been used to a barrier limit as have the tones in our system; in the use of the latter there is little room for further experiment. Composers simply select what they choose from tonal materials, all of which are known. In the "neo" field, there are "neo-romanticists" who turn back to the use of communication and expressiveness as prime factors, after having passed through some sort of "modernism" which had abandoned these factors; there are "neo-modernists" who were once modern, turned neo-classic, and have become modern again. Again, composers are still finding some unexplored aspect to turn back to in classical and earlier music. Stravinsky explores the styles of ancient Greece, early Christian music, Handel, etc., as well as the eighteenth century classic period in music, and has incorporated copious literal quotations, some fairly long, from music by Weber and Tschaikovsky. These actions do not open up more than tiny new horizons, of course; they are a part of the whole spirit of the neo-classical re-evaluation of old styles and means in view of the modern world. There are more recently three strong avenues of approach which open new horizons: one travels toward integration of formerly separate factors (such as classic and modern styles); another draws on musical practises from all over the world; the third makes use of new musical instruments. An obvious possible fourth avenue is not being explored, except by a very few. As experiment in tones has reached the barriers of our tonal system, it is possible to explore in the direction of adding new tones to the system. Quarter tones have been systematized by Alois Hábá of Prague; quarter and eighth tones have been used by Julien Carillo of Mexico; a scale of forty-three unequal tones has been practised by Harry Partch at the University of Wisconsin; but the compositions of these men are worthless, and are written obviously for demonstration purposes only. Charles Ives and Ernest Bloch, both fine composers, make sporadic use of microtones, but not enough to constitute a really determined approach to the subject. The field of microtones, however, may become a wide new horizon before very long, for they may be related to two of the stronger present interests: they are not too hard to perform on some new instruments, and they are a part of some of the non-European music systems, such as the Hindu.

The most successful conservative tendency at present and for the past few years is to integrate old and new musical means. It may seem strange to think of this as offering new horizons, yet the exact materials chosen to place together, and still more important the proportions selected, may produce quite new results. If one mixes an Indian curry with Italian spaghetti sauce, the result is interesting; but it is quite different owing to whether one uses a spoonful of curry in a cup of tomato sauce, or a spoonful of tomato sauce in a cup of curry. So it is in music. There are a number of new flavors produced by mixing the better with the lesser known, and although these flavors are related, each is distinctive. Paul Hindemith is a leader in the field of integration, and some standards of codification for combining diverse elements may be found in his book, *The Craft of Musical Composition.* He specializes in combining elements from Bach and Schoenberg. Prokofiev combined elements from Satie and Stravinsky with mid-nineteenth century models, such as Moussorgsky and Tschaikovsky. Shostakovich, before being enjoined against doing so by the Composer's Union in Russia, tended to spice his music by adding a dash of this and a bit of the other, drawing on all Western European styles rather more eclectically than in an integrated manner. In America a general school of writing has sprung up, using keys and modes a large part of the time, but including some atonality and some chromaticism; using familiar harmonies most of the time, but including some free dissonance and polytonality, using many simple basic rhythms, but with some syncopation and irregularity. This may be said of the work of such successful younger writers as Samuel Barber, Peter Mennin, Norman Dello Joio, David Diamond, and many others. Their styles are more related than separated, yet each produces an individual mixture. Not far removed esthetically are the works of such younger Englishmen as Britten and Rubbra.

As air travel has brought the West within a day or so of the East, and as continuing wars have brought thousands of United Nations men in close contact with the East, its music has been heard and digested by Western people far more than ever before. When Mozart wrote a *Turkish March* there was nothing Turkish about the music; it was just an abstract idea on Mozart's part. He had never heard any

Turkish music. Rimsky-Korsakoff and other nineteenth century Russians heard some music from the Caucasian Mountains, and sometimes quoted bits of it to produce colorful and exotic effects without having the slightest idea that it belongs to an organized system of music. Debussy was greatly stimulated by hearing Javanese and Indo-Chinese music on one occasion only, but it resulted in his building new scales rather than using Oriental ones.

The new horizon, however, is the discovery that Oriental music is not a primitive music, but that each of the important old countries has a highly cultivated musical art, different from each other and from Western art in many respects. These musical arts, accepted by millions of people over hundreds and even thousands of years in some cases, are tried and proved. They have withstood the test of time. Their elements are worthy to be drawn into a more universal art; but it is no longer enough for a Western composer to draw on them rather condescendingly for a bit of atmosphere. He must study intensively for years, know Oriental systems as well as our own, and handle their art so that it is not naive from their standpoint. The Western and Eastern arts must come together on an equal basis. As a whole, Oriental musicians know more of our art than we do of theirs, but it is to be feared that in many cases they underestimate the values in their own musical tradition. A case in point is Japan's well known composer, Yamada, who writes in Western style with a little Japanese color, but does not seem aware of the niceties of the long Japanese musical culture. Some Westerners have learned a great deal about Oriental music. Levis, Fox Strangways, and Kunst have written books on the music of China, India, and Java, respectively; but they are not composers. When Henry Eichheim, a conventional musician who played in the Boston Symphony Orchestra, went to the Orient he was deeply impressed with the music, and came home with many magnificent instruments; but his attempts to use them combined with his own orchestra were weak and without proper knowledge of the Oriental systems.

This horizon is new, and there are many who are interested, few who have as yet been successful. Two men, however, come immediately to mind. Colin McPhee, Canadian born American who lived in Bali for seven years, understands both Western and Balinese music expertly. He was a well known composer before living in Bali; while there he learned the musical system and traditions, and can play on any instrument of the gamelan (Balinese orchestra). His music combining their system with ours seems a complete success. Alan Hovhanness was born in Massachusetts of Armenian parents. He is a thorough student of Armenian traditional music, and has excellent New England training in music of the West. His compositions integrate the two musics extraordinarily well.

The field of experiment with new sounds is almost completely concentrated on *"Musique Concrète,"* in which music is composed directly for a tape recorder. Such experiments were begun within the past five years in France. Facilities of the Paris Radio Station (*Difusion Française*) were made available to Pierre Schaeffer and Pierre Henry, whose compositions, however, seem more for purposes of illustration than works of musical art. However, composers such as Pierre Boulez and Olivier Messiaen have joined the group, and interest has spread to Cologne, Amsterdam, Brussels, and other radio centers. In America an independent movement started, with Edgard Varèse, John Cage, Otto Luening, and Vladimir Ussachevsky working individually along the same lines. While obviously any sort of sound can be recorded on tape, so that quite conventional music could be put together by using ordinary chords and scales, snipping the desired sound from the tapes and joining them together, actually the followers of *Musique Concrète* prefer a wide variety of noises, sometimes mixed with snatches of human voice, in a composed scale of differentiated noise values, so the music is far removed from anything that can be produced otherwise, and far from most people's concept of music.

The creative use of electronic instruments is the newest, most experimental, and in some ways the most sophisticated of the new horizons. On these instruments, control of microtones (those tones which in pitch would lie between the keys of the piano) is fairly easy, so one may predict that as one approaches the horizon of electronics in music, new horizons in the use of microtones may be revealed. This, at least, is one possible future vista.

VIII

NEW HORIZONS IN PAINTING

BY

BEN SHAHN

Do I come to you here as an ambassador from the world of art, to describe to you the bright new horizons that open before us artists, and to leave you with a sense of optimism—a belief that, however dim the morning sun may look upon occasion, all is really basically well in this best of all possible worlds?

If such is the case, then I must indeed be carrying around a chronic kidney ailment, or perhaps I am getting old. There are new horizons, but they lie across despondent swamps and difficult hills that might dampen the courage even of the dauntless Christian of *The Pilgrim's Progress*.

Or perhaps we should reread the old book, and then remember that John Bunyan preferred prison to giving up his right to be a non-conformist, and wonder whether we ourselves have anything like that kind of courage or that kind of conviction.

For non-conformity is precisely what is at issue today, and non-conformity in the field of art presents quite as serious hazards to the well-being of the artist, as does non-conformity in the fields of politics, or religion, or education, or race relations, or any other of those "sensitive" fields wherein such people as you and I carry on most of our existence.

The conformity that is required of us today has little resemblance to the older religious conformity against which John Bunyan struggled so valiantly. The pressures exerted today are less violent than they once were, being now mainly those of social ostracism and loss of livelihood, rather than of imprisonment, torture, or death. But the principle is unchanged; that is, the proscribing of certain kinds of thinking and believing. So, in discussing the present horizons of art, I will first indicate some of the areas of conformity as they exist in the art world.

To the layman, I feel sure that art appears to be in the throes of a great exploratory phase. How else could he explain the strange shapes and forms that it takes today? The average man of goodwill, not wishing to condemn without understanding, tells himself, I believe, that as he is not familiar with the new language of art, he should not sit in judgment upon it.

In fact, the exploratory period out of which our contemporary forms have emerged, occurred some quarter to a half-century ago, and in Europe rather than in America. At that time, new discoveries in optics had made a re-examination of the whole attitude toward color and shape almost mandatory for the artist.

And then, besides being mandatory, it was to be a great and exciting adventure. All the old structures of art, all the old theories began to be re-examined; every accepted rule of perspective, of color, and of perception itself was called into question. The art activity became an exploration of all the possible effects and sensations that can be communicated by way of pictures.

In addition to the new science of optics, another science emerged in the late nineteenth century, one that had tremendous implications for art—the new science of psychoanalysis. And art plunged into an exploration of the sub-conscious and of its various manifestations, that was hardly surpassed by that of the great doctors themselves.

So, toward the end of that century, the beginning of this, pure color and pure form had already widely replaced the true-to-nature colors and forms of traditional art. Psychological material had begun to replace the classical, religious, moral, and romantic subject matter of the academies. Art itself ceased to look like anything that had ever existed before.

That tumultuous period of revolt and rediscovery is assuredly one of the greatest eras of free expression that the art world has ever known. It would be impossible to predict whether the art that came of it will continue to hold a high place in the aggregate panorama of world art. I myself believe that it will endure; for it was serious, it was full of discovery and belief and great new meanings.

As to the impact upon the average man made by this new art, it at first outraged him. But gradually, as is the way with new ideas, it has gained increasing acceptance. And the average man today, whether he knows it or not, has had a wealth of color, form, and design brought into his life directly as a result of the art explorations of the period.

The foregoing indicates something of the background of contemporary American art. But the forms and figures developed during the exploratory period have now formed our horizons. An academy has grown around them which becomes increasingly rigid and intolerant of growth. Those artists who do not conform to its outlook are neglected both by critics and by galleries. Their economic status as artists is in great jeopardy and they are from time to time subjected to most unwarranted attacks as Leftists, Marxists, or some other opprobrious term that has nothing to do with art.

Walter Abel, one of our most knowing art commentators, has divided the characteristic forms of this present day art movement into three categories which he calls, "The Maze," "The Monster," and "The Order." The first of these, "The Maze," began in Germany a number of years ago with the flamelike forms painted by Kandinsky, and with the delicate, imaginative traceries of Paul Klee. It is a much practised art in America today, its most extreme practitioners being Jackson Pollack and possibly Mark Tobey, besides their numerous followers both in and out of the art schools. To the observer such "mazes" present a surface of almost undecipherable forms—or simply of paint drippings—variety within uniformity. The effect sought is a full orchestration of colors and minute shapes or lines, with details kept subordinate to the whole.

"The Monster," Abel's second category, is theoretically the demon of our psychoses (assuming that we have such psychoses). It is the wild horse of our nightmares, the fragmentary human being, the distorted, undefined figure that we almost grasp, and then lose; and besides these phantoms, the objects, the wisps of clothing, that half appear in dreams and hallucinations, and then reshape themselves into unfamiliar forms. Picasso's demonic figures are of this sort of imagery, as are the oversmooth creatures of Dali's canvases. In America, we have Rufino Tamayo, Paul Burlin, and quite a number of other artists who work in such a vein.

"The Order," third of Abel's categories, suggests abstractions such as the cold rectangles of Mondriaan, the abstractions, once developed by Picasso, or the metallic forms of Léger. American Abstractionists are too numerous to mention, but certainly our most conspicuous one is Stuart Davis. "The Order" represents an effort to analyze objects—or just space—into related and essential parts. There are, from time to time, new developments within abstract art, but by far the greater part of it is devoted to monotonous reiteration of already familiar forms.

Such categories by no means cover all the kinds of imagery that enter into contemporary American art. They overlook the so-called "humanistic" current, which is not only our older tradition, but is one that gives some signs of reawakening. But these categories do indicate the general directions of present day art, and also the degree to which it recapitulates the earlier European movements.

Within the past few years the public horizons with regard to art have undergone considerable change. Art schools are thriving everywhere and are developing some professional artists and an enormous number of interested amateurs. Lectures and symposia are on the increase, often dealing with such fine points as the relationship between art and esthetics, or, as the *New York Times* once worded its title, "The Relaxation of Art and Morals." All the conflicting viewpoints on art are being generously aired. And the surprising aspect of all this is the enthusiasm and wide attendance with which the public receives such discussions.

Museums everywhere carry on intensive art activities. Appreciation courses and teaching projects for adults and for children flourish. Today the old lady who takes up painting is no longer looked upon as a bit touched in the head. She is accepted respectfully, and her pictures are likely to command interest (and sometimes high prices). The businessman no longer considers it sissy to visit art galleries, and perhaps even to buy a picture or two. Popular magazines not infrequently carry articles about this or that artist along with handsome full color reproductions of his work. *Time* magazine, which most certainly has its fingers upon the pulse of the nation, carries an art page or two as a regular department.

And on the other hand, the imagery of art has, as I have mentioned, grown ever more removed, cryptic, and abstruse. One is at a loss to explain why it is that, as more and more people become interested in art, art itself seems to grow less and less interested in people.

Recently, there have occurred to me several possible fundamental reasons for this seeming contradiction. In the first place, the patronage of art has undergone a change. For almost a decade—during the thirties—the government was almost the only patron of art. Under its subsidies painting and sculpture matured from an almost unreal, a random sort of occupation, to a major production. Young people who, minus government patronage, might only have dabbled a little in paint, and then have gone on to other, more secure kinds of occupation, now became fulltime artists. Through the eight to ten years of government subsidy, they secured experience and training such as no private school or patronage could ever hope to achieve. Subject matter reflected the patron; because the government itself, during that period was deeply concerned with depression problems, so was the art. Paintings, sculptures, and murals of the thirties were mainly engaged in remembering the Forgotten Man.

But in the early forties, government subsidies were gradually withdrawn. And there existed a sizable population of artists, many of them highly competent and almost all of them without any new outlet for their work. Private galleries began to appear, each seeking to establish some distinguishing trend in art as its own—something more knowing and *advant garde* with which to impress critics and public. Thus the new outlet, the gallery, set the new pace; competitive in the extreme, and competitive on the basis of rarity, the advanced look, the special knowledge required to understand its art. Each trend developed its small circle of admirers who were complaisant in their mastery of the final riddles of art, and were exceedingly hostile to those other groups who had their own sorts of special knowledge and special vocabulary. One might hesitate to compare these latter day art groups with the ancient sects of the Gnostics, but there is, in their tendency to mysticism, and their dependence upon special vocabularies, some little likeness.

There is a further reason—one that might be called an essentially democratic one—for the tendency of art to be non-objective and contentless today. I have mentioned the great enthusiasm of the public for learning how to paint. But it is not easy to become an accomplished artist in the traditional sense. It takes a great deal of hard work, an unavoidable period of struggle and striving in order just to learn to draw a man, a horse, a collection of glasses on a table. It is not easy to compose a crowd; it is not easy to create a series of buildings in perspective—in fact, it is exceedingly difficult. To master the control of painting media is equally arduous; and most difficult of all is to gain ease and virtuosity within a personal style of one's own. Yet all this and much more are the basic prerequisites of the classical art education. Thus any sort of art that does not require so long or so intensive a training period will be welcome to the casual student, as well as to his teacher.

Almost anyone can learn to put together colors, shapes, and lines—to execute a fairly creditable non-objective piece within a relatively brief period of time. If the same student were to essay compositions involving figures, carefully controlled media and emphasis, and so on, his limitations would become glaringly conspicuous. So one must admit that the art which deals only with line, color, and form, while it may have abandoned human beings as subject matter, has at least made it possible for many more of them to paint.

There is another possible reason for the non-objective approach today. Art that is involved with people and purposes, ideas, points of view, and destinies, inevitably enters into areas of controversy. The more penetrating an artist's observation of society, the more likely it is that he will step upon its toes, somewhere; that he will be to some extent a critic of the *status quo*. The *status quo* is more than ordinarily precious in America today. Whoever satirizes it, questions it, or can be construed as questioning it, may find himself in the arms of a committee. Artists, even museum officials, have already had their bout with committees, and certainly the average artist—or layman—

would almost prefer to remain non-committal than to undergo the ordeal of question and suspicion.

Such a climate alone, without the other trends and influences that I have mentioned, would be quite sufficient to chill any very free expression in art, or any very ardent pursuit of the humanistic truths and realities. That sort of painting and sculpture which deals only with patterns, textures, colors, that is, in other words, wholly preoccupied with material and technique, is possibly the most non-committal expression possible to art. I recall, for instance, a certain exhibition that was organized for circulation abroad, in which case it was expressly stipulated that the paintings be abstract and non-objective for the stated reason that such art is non-controversial.

All of which brings us back to the matter of non-conformity; to the fact that it is non-conformity which is under fire today: to our need to face a new outlook. For the freedom to examine honestly; to pursue truth; the freedom to criticize; all these basic conditions for a good society as well as for a meaningful art output have imperceptibly slipped away from us. In this sense, the horizons for art are not separate from the common horizon.

I spoke at the beginning of this discussion about certain "far horizons" for art that lie across some rather difficult terrain. I have tried to indicate some of the problems that possibly stay the advance of art, such as that of the de-emphasizing of training, of the need to be *avant garde,* the specialness of the art market, and then the climate of suspicion in which the artist must work.

But art has a certain Phoenixlike character. Whenever it has suffered a decline—and it has suffered many such declines during past times—it seems to stir in its ashes and reappear, vigorous and ready to tell man new things about reality. Possibly it is from the very needs of society itself that art derives its renewed vigor: for it is of the very essential character of art that it seeks new value, that it attaches itself to belief and conviction. Those virtues, and beliefs, and refinements which civilization holds most dear are inseparably interwoven with the images of art, which has both followed and led in the slow process of informing, educating, and civilizing man.

I do not think that that capacity has run out, any more than the human need for a sort of spiritual, imaginative reassurance has run out. It is within the new needs of man that the new horizons for art will be found. And if I were to predict more closely, I would say that the next turn that art takes may see a re-emphasis of the full human being, including his capacities to think well, to believe, to have compassion for his fellows, and to express freely whatever truths he finds.

IX

WHAT HAS THE THEATER TO OFFER?[1]

BY

WALTER KERR

When I was invited to take part in this series I was instructed to conduct myself in an entirely informal although quite specific manner. I am going to violate, I am afraid, one of these charges, the charge about being quite specific. I am going to tell you why.

I do think that the time has come for new horizons in the theater. I think the old one has receded almost to infinity, as our audiences have receded to infinity.

I think the cause is something as simple as this: theatrical activity is not a steady, continuous movement over the centuries. We are not a part and parcel of something that started in Greece. Rather, all theatrical activity operates in lively short term cycles. We tend to think of ourselves as belonging to a pattern that began with Sophocles and to which we are closely attached. Actually the theater of Sophocles and Euripides was over and done with in seventy years.

The theater of Shakespeare, the greatest we have had in English, was over in forty-two years. No theatrical cycle—a given impulse, a given way of mirroring ourselves as we see ourselves—has ever endured in the theater for more than seventy years, for more than the life of the oldest inhabitant sitting in the theater.

Our own cycle today is seventy years old. It begins with Ibsen and Chekhov. Any play that Arthur Miller writes is an Ibsen play. We continue to have Chekhovian plays, muted studies of character in a kind of narrative void. Both of these forms are aged. They have, I think, lost their initial vitality. I think they reflect a way of life and

[1] This chapter is based on a stenotype record rather than a manuscript.

103

an attitude toward life which, as a matter of fact, is now dead. And I think because they are still reflecting attitudes which have lost impetus, we are no longer able to go to the theater and see ourselves in the theater and, therefore, we are no longer eager to go to the theater.

That is why we are, to a great extent, bored with the contemporary theater, and our boredom accounts for the shrinkage which has been increasing over a long period of time. I think a cycle is dead. Therefore, obviously and clearly, we need a new horizon. What that new horizon is going to be I, of course, cannot tell you. No one can say precisely what fundamental underground forces are now at work which will heave to the surface in a short time, which we will recognize as being our new impulses and new attitudes toward ourselves and our culture, which we will come to want to see on the stage because this is what we think of ourselves as being. Obviously we are going through a time of transition, forming new attitudes toward the world, toward ourselves, toward our relationship to the world, and when these become sufficiently formulated in our own minds for a playwright to detect them, he will begin to put them on the stage. I think we will then have a new variation on an old universality. I cannot anticipate that variation so I am going to have to speak generally.

Though we are in a time of transition we must at least consider in general terms the possible future or what we can do, if anything, toward the possible future. Therefore, let us alter the question to ask what, in that possible future is the theater likely to have to offer.

First of all to state what the theater does not have to offer, the theater does not offer to religion, to sociology, to politics a relief from their own burdens. In other words, I am very much opposed to an attitude toward the theater which holds it to be a packass on which the difficulties and disappointments and sometimes even despairs of other human activity can be loaded.

If I start out on such a negative note, it is because we have been passing through a time—we are not quite out of it yet—where the theater, and the other arts as well, have been asked to take on this kind of burden, have been asked to offer this kind of assistance to all of our other cultural media. We have been asked in the theater to offer artificial respiration to media which are gasping. We have regarded the theater not essentially as pleasure or as play, but as a tool of useful work. We have asked it to do useful work which was not being done, I think, in other and rather more relevant channels.

For example, in our time politics has asked of the theater that it debate political issues, that the theater direct men's minds into certain liberal political courses, that the theater arouse audiences to actual political activity. I would like to note that this insistence that the theater do these things coincides precisely with the decline of a stump rhetoric, with a decline in the quality of public debate, with the decline of the passionate political caucus. We have almost no passion in our political meetings today. The only time we see any passion is at the two national conventions, and one knows how artificial, how utterly mechanical that excitement is. Because passion is called for we whip some up. Genuine passion, the notion that people might with passion assemble for a political meeting, a political debate, a political gathering has largely disappeared from our lives. In short, as political activity has lost its own power of direct appeal, it has in a sense asked the theater with its own peculiar perennial appeal to take over.

Religion has asked in a much weaker, slightly defensive and certainly less effective way, that the theater assume certain of its burdens. We still hear, and rather frequently, such things as, "Look at the Godless plays about us. We must counterattack immediately by writing Catholic plays, producing Protestant movies," and so on. We encourage views which link the drama and the church, which point to their common origins. We make a great deal of this. We speak about the influence for "good" which the drama might have. We may say—I may not be able to write it without offense—that our present interest in having the theater and the other arts take on any of this obligation coincides with a decline in pulpit rhetoric, in the arts of moral persuasion as practised by the clergy.

Sociology has been most successful in transferring certain of its obligations to the theater, particularly its obligation to popularize new social concepts. And, of course, the theater has taken on this burden and has popularized for us concepts of environment and heredity and so on which have been put forth endlessly over the past seventy or eighty years.

Because sociology is a new science it is going to be difficult for me to show that its effort coincides with the decline in past performance. But if a sociologist is to impress his vision upon the minds of men, he surely has an obligation to write well, and we cannot say that contemporary sociology, with its fondness for jargon, writes well. The notion of the man of science who is also a man of letters, the abstract thinker who also writes beautifully, has disappeared from our society, and we come close to saying, "Let the thinker think and let the theater spread the thought."

As these various instruments toward the common good—the pulpit, the stump, and the scientist who can write—have progressively lost their power of communication, the theater and the other arts have been asked to communicate for them. That is one reason why today we are constantly being asked to call all arts "communication" arts. The phrase has a hollow sound, but it is a commonplace phrase among us.

One curious thing about the theater or any other art that has become a communication art (carrying the burden of communicating other men's voices) is that the audience does not care much about going to it, and the decline which has set in in our theater, which I partially attributed to the end of a cycle, really began at precisely the time when the theater was asked to assume these burdens. It is with the beginning of the theater of Ibsen and Chekhov that the audience begins to leave the theater, and it has left it progressively year by year ever since. In other words, as the theater has assumed alien burdens the audience has in precise proportions drifted away. I suspect the audience is right. The audience has an intuitive understanding of the fitness of the tool for its proper work—it wants preaching from priests, politics from politicians, and sociology from men who have actually been trained in one or another science—and it does seem to ask something else of the theater.

Our focus in this series ought to be on the relationship between religion and the theater and our special question ought to be: "What demands may religion make of the theater in the new horizons toward which we are theoretically moving?" The relationship of religion and drama, of course, is an extremely old one. It has always been an extremely uneasy one—old but unhappy. For instance, we are very fond of recalling that drama always began in some sort of religious exercise, or seemed to. We like to remember that the Greek drama began with the dithyramb that it came out of an actual religious rite: we like to remember that when drama had to be reborn, it came out of the Mass in medieval times. These things are true, historically speaking, and we can go back and look at them and see a close relationship.

In our enthusiasm we like to forget certain things. We forget the atmosphere which prevailed once this monster had been born of religion. One of the things you will find in looking back is that a man like Archilochus, who was very good at leading the Greek religious dithyramb, was especially good at it when he was drunk. Or we might look at the medieval drama and quickly discover it to have been the object of endless complaint. Once drama had been born of the religious ritual, it seems immediately to have led to "boisterousness and laxity" in church. And we know from subsequent history, that though the medieval church seems to have given birth to our drama, it had to kick that drama down the front steps of the cathedral rather rapidly. It simply had to.

We seem then to owe drama to religion, but yet the two have never been held in any kind of stable relationship. We may say that there are two results of too close an intimacy, too close a relationship between these things. First, the art itself does not mature so long as it is held in its original environment. We have an excellent example in the three to four hundred years of medieval drama. During this period the church still had a very firm hold on the drama and put it to very specific church uses. And during that time, although the entire society was fascinated by this tool, although the church itself set aside holidays for the presentation of these plays, although every citizen was taxed for the support of these plays—a situation we have not come to here—although everything financial and popular was geared to the development of this thing for a very long time, not a single major work of art was produced. In other words, not until it skipped off, went away, got out of the church, did the drama begin to mature; then it matured rather rapidly. Art itself does not seem to mature while it is too closely held in the environment.

Secondly, religion itself is distressed so long as any real intimacy prevails. We seem to have a permanent uneasiness about drama. Religion feels bound to claim it because it gave it birth, but to regard it as suspect because it ran away. A tension exists (instinctive affection, rueful hostility) because drama behaved in so ungrateful a fashion. We would like to get back into some kind of settled, easier relationship with it.

Generally speaking, the best we can think of is to try to absorb it functionally; that is, make it serve our function, ask that it treat religious subject matter, ask that it inculcate a formulated moral lesson, ask that it provide a specifically religious experience. This last, by the way, seems an extremely dangerous request. The moment you convince people that the experience of art is a specifically religious one, you are going to find people substituting art for religious experience. You do find it now in a great many quarters.

The practise leads to the kind of statement Maxwell Anderson is fond of making. Mr. Anderson likes to think of the theater as "the temple of democracy," with the clear implication that there is no other temple adequate to a democracy. So there is a danger involved there. But if the theater is not a substitute for religion and if it never behaves itself in the precincts of religion, how does it happen to take its impulse from religion?

There are several different ways of looking at the matter. I will have to tread cautiously here, for I should not be talking to you about religion. Nevertheless, there are a couple of suggestive things that might be said. One of them is this. Religion, after all, decreed the time for play, in the beginning. It was religion which allowed for play. Even by the simple fact of setting aside one day from work it suggested, even when it did not explicitly state, that that day was a day for relaxation and for recreation.

Secondly, it was religion that created the opportunity and the occasion for group activity—drama of course is a group activity among

the arts—by calling men together from their separate work pursuits
for the purpose of worship in assembly. It brought them into an assembly, and when the worship was completed, the assembly, on a
day free from work, went on to engage in group play. That is quite
clear in the Greek instance.

Almost from the very beginning you have instances of play in the
Greek religious exercise. You know from the beginning that costumes
were used, and that dance was an integrated portion of the ritual.
You also know that drunkenness was common, that ribaldry was
common, and, as someone has said, very often the success of one of
the Greek religious rites was measured by the number of babies born
nine months afterward. I suggest there is a play element involved in
any religious ritual which produces this sort of result.

We can watch, for instance, the Greek altar itself shifting, losing
its value, and becoming finally a theatrical prop, a prop for play. The
religious center tended to become a theatrical center in a playful
activity. Furthermore, in Greek history this religious occasion did
become a public holiday. The same thing happened in the medieval
instance. In fact, it is perpetuated to this day. Most Catholics go to
Mass in the morning and have some kind of fun in the afternoon,
whether they go to the movies, go out and meet friends, or play ball.
The pattern of worship and play, the relationship of these two things,
continues. The medieval feast day is in the very term, "feast," an indication of the close association of these two things in which we cele-
brate the Mass first and freedom from labor second. The procession
tends to become a parade.

I think in the negative sense, too, if I understand this correctly, the
point is made even clearer by the Jewish instance. There play or sport
was forbidden on the day of worship. In this case drama did not
develop. That is to say, though you still have the religious rite present,
because you do not have the permission to play the art form does not
grow in the environment.

We actually may say then that drama did not come naturally from
a religious exercise when the religious exercise was separated from
play.

And we may finally see why Thomas Aquinas always talked about the arts in terms of play, always talked about the arts in terms of pleasure, although he lived and wrote at a time when the medieval experiment of treating drama as a tool was decidedly under way. Aquinas, as you know, says that the object of play acting is "to cheer the heart of man." "If man cannot have intellectual pleasures, the pleasures of the spirit, he will seek the pleasures of the flesh." He gave the definition always in terms of pleasure, intellectual pleasure. The activity is also described as play.

These three cases, the Greek, the medieval, and the Jewish, seem to suggest, both positively and negatively, that the origin of drama is not precisely in the religious rite itself but in the occasion for mass play which the rite sometimes creates. Are we to conclude from this (and it is a very superficial examination) that our long standing belief that there is some kind of intimate connection between drama and religion is wholly false? I do not think so.

I think there is another way of looking at it, but here I am going to have to speak figuratively or analogically. I am going to have to take Genesis as my text, and I am certainly no biblical scholar.

I want to remind you of something else we forget, that before the fall of man in Eden man was in a state of what has been described as perpetual pleasure. It was not just a paradise, it was a paradise of "pleasure"—carefully spelled out. It was not a paradise of labor, of achievement, of information. It was not a vast sociological library. It was a paradise of pleasure.

It was, in fact, precisely when man got a little nosy about certain kinds of information that he was thrown out of this paradise of pleasure. And we must not assume that his pleasure in the Garden was simply physical. We do tend to have a terrible habit today of equating pleasure and physical pleasure. We have come to demean the term terribly. When we think of pleasure today we think of something cheap, we think of something in which an honorable man, a productive man, a useful man in the society does not really indulge. If he does, he is a little embarrassed by it. He certainly never thinks of pleasure as being potentially intellectual. We have degraded the term.

The pleasure of paradise was not simply a paradise of physical pleasure. It must also have been a paradise of intellectual pleasure. What could this mean? It suggests to me that this was a paradise in which man knew things and knew them with delight, with pleasure. Shall we say he must have been able in some way or other to look at God's creation, at created being around him, and love it on sight, pleasurably, certainly without difficulty?

This would seem to have been a simpler, rather more immediate, quickly delightful knowledge of natural being without the precise labor we must undergo now when we want to have knowledge of the things about us. In fact, we are told that when man was expelled from this Garden his understanding was darkened, that is to say, knowledge was not so easy to come by. By the sweat of his brow man would now have to establish a new and much more difficult relation with the universe about him. He would have to forge out a sociology in order to preserve himself. He would have to forge a politics in order to govern himself. He would have to forge, laboriously, a philosophy and a theology, in order to know that God Who had spoken directly to him in the Garden.

But to continue with Genesis, this understanding which man had was darkened, not destroyed; that is to say, it must still have been possible in some dim way and after great difficulty to return to the quickly pleasurable way of knowing things, of knowing created nature, of all that being that is about us and in us. And having returned there, however briefly, however dimly, with whatever difficulty, we would be better off than before. We would not be better off politically because we still have to work that out. We would not be better off socially because we still have to work that out. In the strict sense we would not be better off morally. That is to say, our moral character would not necessarily have been vastly improved by having returned to this kind of delightful knowledge of things. We might, for instance, go on eating apples even after we had been there. But in a loose and still quite genuine sense, we might have been religiously improved in that we had momentarily and inadequately come back to the sort of knowing, the pleasurable knowing which God had in mind for man in the first place and which man himself darkened.

Let us say that we have returned to this intuition, to the delightfully contemplative vision of things as opposed to a laboriously profitable view of things. If our contemplation of creation has been genuine, we cannot help but be delighted with it. But to be delighted we must be willing to sit still like Mary and not to be busy about the household chores like Martha. Mary and Martha both possessed certain kinds of knowledge. They both knew certain necessary things. We need these two attitudes toward the universe today. But the arts, including the theater, seem to me to be essentially Marys. We have lately made them Marthas. We have kept them very, very busy about the household chores, and I think that we have denied them and degraded them and made them unpopular in the course of it.

What has the theater to offer? Not the busy usefulness of Martha, not the tidying up of the social house. It offers love, love of what is seen as simply, as directly, and as accurately as possible. The theater may return to some kind of health when it stops tidying up other men's houses. When the theater returns to some kind of affection for the created universe, a simple, honest affection, willing to leave the universe alone, merely to look at it and see what it is, then some sort of new horizon in the theater may develop.

Going to the theater can never be construed as an act of piety. But surely it is an act which piety helped to bring into existence, an act which piety once approved and might well approve again. It is possibly even an act of which piety may well be proud.

X

ACTUALITIES AND POSSIBILITIES IN TELEVISION

BY

ROBERT SAUDEK

Most of us have some familiarity with the actualities of television—at least, with such a part of it as is visible on the screen. Other parts are hidden from public view, largely because they are not of general interest: such actualities as the means of production and distribution, the costs, the techniques and the methods of buying and selling, the organization of networks and program producing agencies, the policies and the relationships with the government. Yet each of these latter phases of television constitutes an important part of it as an actuality, and may affect its possibilities.

This is a new process. It is the process of transmitting moving images and sound, as they happen, from one point to millions of other points simultaneously.

So quickly has this electronic wonder been made practical that nearly 400 transmitters are actually carrying images into about 28,000,000 homes from early morning until late at night every day in the week. And so attractive are these images—for better or for worse—that some 75,000,000 Americans are spending hours each day watching the creative efforts of those responsible for presenting television programs.

This phenomenon is breathtaking beyond description. It is breathtaking not just for its enormity, nor for the statistical hyperbole it generates, but because the forward thrust of science which has solved basic technical problems, has always far outstripped the ability of creative people to measure up to the humanistic responsibilities which science places in them.

It is as though a physicist had created an auditorium whose architecture and acoustics far surpassed any previous design, and then the community which inherited this masterpiece of sight and sound had been faced with the problem of utilizing it to its full potentiality.

The producers of the programs you see today on television, which I have called only a part of the so-called actuality of contemporary television, have scarcely had time to sit back and reflect on the implications of the medium for which they are responsible. Even those who indulge themselves in the luxury of social research about television fall, one by one, into the trap of measuring existing habits and effects, only to find that their measurements are out of date by the time they are published. Add to this the fact that those who measure do not always create, and all the statistics in the world will not modify the practises which they are measuring.

It takes a different set of muscles and nerves to criticize than it does to create. The one thing which may be common to critic and creator alike is their standard of judgment.

Men and women who are responsible for the programs you watch on television have little time to look beyond this week or this season, to project what they have created against a background of the possibilities of this medium. Scarcely anyone is worrying about where television might be five or ten years from now.

The consequence of this situation is that television programs tend to be safe and sound. They live by moral prohibitions, by "Thou shalt nots." Yet something must be said in defense of the dilemma in which television people find themselves. Unlike the science of television, the art of television is extremely subtle, changeable and is not subject to mathematical proof. It is possible to determine how many millions of viewers watched a given program, but it is impossible to know why they watched, or what was the peculiar combination of experience, taste, and production that appealed to any one of the viewers, let alone all of them individually. Thus, unlike its electronics, television's development as an art form, or an entertainment medium, or a conduit of information is subject only in the most limited sense to growth by trial and error, or by the development of production theories. To catch and preserve and repeat the elements which made a particular program successful, is almost as unrewarding as the attempt to catch and hold and preserve the sparks that fall from a Fourth of July sparkler.

In many respects those of us who are trying to produce programs in this new and boundless medium find ourselves in the position of a small child who receives a Stradivarius on the day of his first violin lesson: he is custodian of a priceless instrument which he is totally incapable of using.

This is an exaggeration for purposes of example. Obviously, many of the people operating today in television have brought to it the traditions of the theater and the motion pictures and radio. There are experts in the field of journalism. But in the rough and tumble processes of putting programs on the air the challenge is to create artistic endeavors which are indigenous to television. In short, what can one do, besides borrowing from other art forms, which will utilize the immense potentialities of a transmission which begins at one point and ends in 28,000,000 points, and can touch, persuade, arouse, alert, awaken 75,000,000 minds? One must not be surprised nor alarmed at the fact that a bare six years of television has not been enough to meet the challenge with full force and effect. It is comforting to recall that six years after the practical utilization of the printing press its effectiveness was limited to perhaps hundreds of people, and the nature of the messages which were reproduced was probably no more original than the manuscripts which immediately preceded that great invention. Artistic techniques took generations to develop. The use of a metal press and reproductions of works of art, the creation of type faces and of formats came not years, but centuries after the invention of the press itself. Measured in these terms television has moved ahead by great strides.

But consider the fallacy of comparison. Today's world, infinitely more complex, highly organized, better educated, more sophisticated in its tastes, naturally expects a more rapid improvement of television than people of the Middle Ages ever expected of the printing press. Having become accustomed to speed, having organized its laws and its life in accordance with rapid transportation and communications, having built an extremely delicate set of mechanisms on which the economy, the science, the construction, and even the destruction of our civilization depends, our generation makes the interesting but erroneous demand for speed in the humanities, which, curiously enough, move at apparently the same pace at which they moved centuries ago. The electronic age, for all its high speed, has yet to produce a William Shakespeare, a Plato, or a Jesus.

May it not then be said that the genius of our age is in its organization to transmit and utilize the ideas of men; but that the ideas of men—their social and political and spiritual and literary ideas—move forward at a predetermined pace unaffected by the scientist, the laboratory, or the manufacturer's production line.

One must speculate on the effect which major advances in the physical sciences may have on the creativity of those engaged in the arts who would naturally fall heir to the utilization of such advances. There is the rather popular theory that the invention of television has had a degrading effect on artistic achievement, in the sense that television has provided an outlet for increasing quantities of mediocre writing, acting, designing, and the like. As uncomplicated as this kind of reasoning may appear to be, it fails to consider the effect which such a medium might have on the small band of creative people for whom the advent of a new medium presents the unexpected delights of reaching new and greater audiences in a new and challenging form of presentation.

One must recall, from Thomas Gray's *An Elegy Written in a Country Churchyard* the lament that "full many a flower is born to blush unseen, and waste its sweetness on the desert air." Would it not seem that, as new ways of communicating ideas present themselves, fewer flowers need to remain unseen or waste their sweetness? Television is a form, and the things which are carried by it are the substance. It is generally true that the creation of form brings behind it the creation of substance. A good form inspires good substance, and the converse is likewise true. Applied to other fields, when a worthy form of government was afforded our country in 1787, the substantive ways of life which eventually flowed from that fountainhead made a great contribution to civilization, although the full force of our

Constitution was by no means felt during the first decade or even two decades of its existence.

Curiously enough, when a mischievous framework is created, as in the case of a totalitarian state, the substantive outgrowth of law and custom is soon apparent, and its intolerable effects, like a cancer, multiply themselves rapidly and by geometric progression.

I suppose it must be stated, in all objectivity, that at this early stage of television it is not yet possible to judge whether this form which science has created is a good or bad form, and therefore whether the effect of the material being created for it is generally running in the direction of gain or loss to our culture.

However, there are healthy cells which one does not ordinarily find in cancerous growths. If we can accept as a fact the extreme youthfulness of television, and as a second fact its hyperthyroid growth which has made it a man long before its time, then we may examine this youth for signs of strength and character. Within this context it is not essential, and in fact it would be most unsympathetic to youth, to expect the full flowering of the qualities which constitute greatness or even goodness. But if, when youth is put to the periodic tests of character and resourcefulness, of natural sensitivity and responsiveness, it is not found wanting, its awkwardness and its irritating flamboyances may be excused.

This is the greatest hope for television. There have been times in the recent past when this youthful child has had to face the responsibilities of manhood, and there have been times when it has responded with nobility and sacrifice. One recalls great events which have been reported faithfully and with dignity by the television cameras. One recalls the dedication with which some of our best writers have turned to television as they did *not* turn to radio, and have expended themselves generously. One must know of the demands which television has placed upon good designers who have been called to create a veritable multitude of artistic creations in the television studios, and who have driven their imaginations beyond any goals which either the theater or the motion pictures have expected of them. In the field of performance, celebrated actors and actresses whose reputations have long since been secure have risked themselves once more in a precarious field which asks them to memorize many different plays in the course of a season, and expects of them a patience during camera rehearsals which is unmatched by any other theatrical medium. Yet many of the great personalities of the stage have come to television again and again with little expectation of any artistic rewards, but with bountiful gifts which they can bring to numberless audiences.

There are men engaged in television who have had such respect for the dimensions of this new medium that they have either withheld themselves from it until they had something to say and a proper way to say it, or who have come into television for smaller financial rewards than they might enjoy elsewhere, just because of the ideal with which television seemed to present them. Such a person is Edward R. Murrow, and more recently Elmer Davis.

A fourth test of the potential strength of television is its ability to support the great works of the past, without so mutilating them that they become an apology for their own greatness. Television has at least made the attempt. It has undertaken with great seriousness of purpose to perform the works of Shakespeare, to interpret the Bible, to project the novels and short stories of some of the world's finest authors. In so doing it has occasionally tried to discover new ways of telling these tales, ways that might have been embraced by authors and playwrights of the past if they had had the opportunity to create originally for the medium of television rather than that of the stage or the printed page. This is a precarious and often presumptuous undertaking, but it must not be confused with exhibitionism.

If all of what I have said were to be heard by a visitor from some remote desert island he might have the impression that American television today is a horn of plenty, rich in the works of past and living masters, punctuated by a wealth of special features involving science, the news, and our social and artistic heritage. He might believe that American television is a combination of Carnegie Hall, the Empire Theater, the great universities, and a front row seat in the United States Supreme Court. This is neither the present situation nor the future prospect. Television will always be bigger than the

ability to fill it with great works. It might even be said that television
will be able to afford to do some great things only so long as more
than half of its output is popular enough to attract large audiences
whose primary interests in life are not intellectual interests.

Thus, I am led to the inevitable conclusion that television's influence may be measured by the dual standard of its popular appeal and
its intellectual appeal. Ideally, these appeals must not, I believe, run
in parallel lines to infinity. They must both touch the same wide
audience, and to that extent, television's intellectual efforts may
always be subject to a snobbish accusation of artistic compromise.

There is among the critics of television a smouldering conflict
which only occasionally bursts into open flame. On one side are those
who would take television unto themselves and use it for increasingly
intellectual pursuits on the theory that a medium of these proportions
deserves nothing but the best and the finest. There is another group,
with which I would identify myself, which believes that television is
something of a reflection of life itself, and that life itself is not, for most
people, made up of a series of intellectual pursuits. The fact that
a well integrated life includes many relatively unimportant activities,
reactions, and feelings, that it involves, like the flow of blood through
the heart, surges of momentum and pressure alternating with times
of relaxation, may be said to be as good a reason as any to pattern
such a time and talent consuming medium as television to the pattern
of the life around us.

When men are incapable of turning their full time and strength to
the production of great works in their lives, they generally find it
possible to live usefully by living at all times honorably, and at some
times with unusual force and meaning. Television, beset as it is by
some of the tribulations which human beings face—the trials of
economics, of a lack of imagination, or of attention to details which
involve such mechanical things as schedules—may do its best by
devoting its greatest strength to those times when a combination of
ideas, ideals, and the will to transform them into good works come
together in the television studio. If one accepts this much of the
concept, then one must move forward to the challenge that lies in
that part of television which would demand great inspiration and

great effort. In the formative years of this medium the challenge further implies the continued broadening of the area of television to be treated with such respect and effort.

Heretofore it has been generally believed that the way to sell goods and services by television was to lower the level of television. In the past two years my colleagues and I have been engaged in an effort to prove that it is also possible to sell goods and services by raising the level of television. Whether or not this case has been proved, it is clear that a number of such forces have recently been at work in television and have, among them, added considerable evidence to the case for this theory. Never in the history of radio was such a concerted effort made. Only now, in the waning years of radio, are those air waves filled with more and more good music and good discussion, but the impetus came from economics and not from the arts.

It would be unfair for me to predict that the possibilities in television are essentially cultural, or that all of it could ever be raised to the standards maintained, for example, by this Institute for Religious and Social Studies or other organizations similarly dedicated. It may be said, however, that yeast is present in this new medium in the form of a great variety of talents which have no intention of allowing television to become a mediocrity. Cynicism is the easiest and laziest of philosophies, requiring no positive action, no dynamics and no hope. Those who apply to all of television's present and future the flaws which they find in it, either in its product or its structure, would not be satisfied in their hearts if television brought them an all day diet of chamber music, fine arts, and philosophical discourse. On the other hand, chronic cynicism represents an unhealthy state of mind and no enterprise seeking ways to improve must measure itself by unhealthy standards of judgment.

Watchfulness must be the responsibility of men and women who know that the artistic and moral development of any medium can go only at a pace consistent with the artistic and moral development of human beings and their society. This rate of development bears no relationship to that which characterizes scientific achievement. Instead, it is made up of tolerance, encouragement, and criticism, on the one hand, and prodding, goading, and leadership on the other.

If the possibilities for raising the level of television have not yet been exhausted, then it is incumbent on this generation to devote the greater part of its attention to the realization of these possibilities, which, as they are accomplished, will reduce accordingly that portion of television which is today characterized by mediocrity.

XI

NEW ART AND OLD MORALS

BY

W. G. CONSTABLE

During the past half century there has developed, notably among artists, renewed concern as to the spiritual and moral influence of the arts. The view that the main business of the arts is with beauty and the stimulating of pleasurable feelings, has to a considerable extent fallen into the background, and its place has been taken by a conception of art as a means of knowing and as a source of inspiration. This has been recognized and acted upon in strange quarters. Totalitarian governments have taken drastic steps to regulate the kind of art produced in their several countries; the Roman Catholic Church has revealed itself as highly suspicious of some contemporary movements in painting and sculpture; and even in the United States, certain kinds of painting, despite being exactly those denounced and banished by Hitler and Stalin, have been abused as being subversive and as propaganda for Communism.

The art against which these attacks have been directed is what has come to be called "modern," which can perhaps best be defined as the art which finds a welcome in the Museum of Modern Art; a dominant characteristic of which is rejection of the conventions of the past, and the search for new kinds of forms and arrangements of forms to express the artist's feelings. One objection of totalitarians to such art is that it is not easily understood by what they call the "average man," and so is defective for propaganda purpose. Another, and more serious is that even when only dimly grasped, such art is liable to make men think and to question established values, something totalitarians do not like.

123

Certainly, the artists themselves and their apologists give plenty of color to this second objection. The tendency today is to exalt the spiritual potentialities of the arts. A work of art may not only have a sensuous emotional appeal, and make severe demands upon the intellect, but may also call into play the imagination, thereby moving into what has been well called the supra-intellectual field, in which rational considerations yield to direct cognition, as in the case of the religious mystic and the great mathematician. So mind and emotions may be set to work by the revelation of truths, which, like many of those of religion and mathematics, are at present unprovable. Needless to say, there are many works of art which do not, and whose makers would not claim for them, this power. Even the best designed chair does not offer the spiritual possibilities of Hagia Sophia; but this does not negative the existence of those possibilities.

This conception of art is no new thing, but has been proclaimed in the past both by artists and writers on art. All that is new, is that it has been given greater precision by modern psychologists. Taking it as a startingpoint, the next step is to consider the relation of art, and especially of modern art, to morals, a term which I use here in the sense of ethics and not of *mores*—a code of right and wrong and not of manners. At once the vexed question arises of the origins and sanctions of moral codes. It has, for example, been denied that there is any necessary connection between ethics and religion. Fortunately, that question demands no answer here, and it can be assumed that man's spiritual state is at least likely to influence his moral code; so that art, through its spiritual influence, may well affect morals.

Artists and writers on art, however, have gone further, and have claimed and claim today for art a direct moral influence, both by example and precept. Some, indeed, have gone farther, and hold that unless an art promotes good morals, it is not good art. This last view is that of classical antiquity, in whose mind the good and the beautiful were so closely linked as to be inseparable. Plato banned what he calls the "art of imitation" from his Republic, on the ground that it imitated appearance which was itself an imitation, and so was "the worthless mistress of a worthless friend and the parent of a worthless progeny." In other words, as Plato's conception of art gave it no moral value, he rejects art. Aristotle rates the artist as of greater importance; but measures his merit by a moral yardstick, in judging work according to whether it makes man appear more beautiful and more noble than in fact he is. Apparently this view squared with artists' practise, for Polygnotus is said to have subordinated technique to moral qualities, such as dignity and grandeur in conception and the portrayal of greatness of character.

The conception that the artist's business is to realize an ideal toward which nature is always working, but will never realize, and that he should express moral sentiments, is one that appears and reappears constantly throughout the history of art. During the Renaissance, for example, it takes various forms. Michelangelo, whose writings give a more nearly precise account of his aims than we possess for any other great artist, sought for an ideal beauty which was beyond that of nature and was a reflection of the divine in a material world; while in his later work, his search for expression of a Christian piety was so intense, that at the last he renounces the arts for religion. With Michelangelo, the influence of art on morals was implied rather than expressed; but in Savonarola's denunciation of the art of his time, a direct connection is stressed.

It was, however, in the seventeenth and the eighteenth century that the notion of the ideal in art and of art's moral obligations, took definite form. Painting and poetry were regarded as sister arts, as expressed in the Horatian tag, *"ut pictura poesis."* Painting, like poetry, must point a moral, and concern itself with lofty themes and great men. So came to be established a hierarchy of painting according to the subject, headed by what was called "history" painting, occupied with heroic themes from the past, with still life at the bottom; the order being determined by the subjects' capacity for moral improvement.

Even where the treatment was sternly realistic, the same rule held good. After the Council of Trent, the great orders of the Church used paintings with the most savage and revolting subjects, both to warn and to edify; Diderot, perhaps the most perspicacious critic of the eighteenth century, praised the paintings of peasant life by Greuze, for their moral influence; and Jacques Louis David, a man of the

French Revolution and its painter, a realist to the core, deliberately chose his subjects to inculcate revolutionary virtues. Even John Constable, founder of modern landscape painting, who found inspiration in the quieter beauties of the English countryside, justly claimed his work to be poetic, with the Wordsworthian implication that to be poetic was to be moral.

In the nineteenth century, however, the moral aim receded into the background. Partly this was due to the influence of German speculation. A succession of writers, notably Lessing, Winckelmann, and Goethe, held that the conception of the beautiful could be separated from that of the good, and that art was concerned with the beautiful. In other words, the merits of a work of art were not necessarily dependent on its moral effect. Meanwhile, a social revolution of the first magnitude was taking place in Western Europe. The last stage of the Industrial Revolution had begun, coal and iron were in the saddle, and factory organization the rule. The old supremacy of courts and of a territorial nobility, were being challenged by an industrial and commercial aristocracy, while the influence of working people was increasing.

The influence on the arts was twofold. In the first place, the sources of patronage were changing. The new patrons, less well educated, less sophisticated, and less influenced by tradition than the old, wanted an art they could understand; so the importance of heroic subject matter declined, and genre, landscape and still life took its place, with emphasis on reproducing appearance. The significance of this is far greater than it may seem at first sight. From now onward, subject lost its importance as a means of conveying moral instruction; while the aim of idealizing human nature, and so setting up a moral standard, virtually disappeared. Secondly, the social revolution involved a widening gulf between artists and the rest of the community. Art, which under older regimes had been treated as part and parcel of the everyday world, tended in the new world of industry and commerce to be regarded as something esoteric, with which most people had nothing to do; and thus the artist became isolated from daily life. At the same time, the Romantic movement laid increasing emphasis on art being less a means of communication than one of self-expression, and that what the artist produced was his business, and not that of the public; whence it followed that art had no concern with morals, other, perhaps, than those of the artist.

These tendencies found full development in the work of the Impressionist painters, and in the doctrine of Art for Art's Sake. The core of Impressionist theory and practise is that the painter's material is what the eye sees, not what the mind knows; and because it is light which enables us to see, the Impressionist is primarily a painter of light. So subject, except as a means of reflecting light, is unimportant; and any connection of painting with morals is irrelevant.

Clearly, the conception of Art for Art's Sake justified Impressionist practise; but it went further than this. It has often been assailed as a denial of moral restraint, and a justification for loose living; in fact, it was a declaration of freedom for the artist. It met the disregard of the artist by society, by the claim that the artist should be left to work as he thought best; while at the same time emphasizing the paramount importance of art to the moral and spiritual health of man. It followed therefore that whatever the artist judged good as art, was good for other people.

Thus, once more the age old contention became current that art and morals are inseparable, though in a different form. The art was not to be measured against the morals, but the morals against the art. William Morris went the whole way with this. For him, the work of the artist was *per se* good; and if society could not benefit from art, then society must be changed. Ruskin and Tolstoy rebelled, however. Both accepted the necessity of art, and paid lip service to freedom for the artist; but both held that the artist must trim his activity to fit the moral code of his day. Ruskin could say "life without industry is guilt, and industry without art is brutality"; but later added "you must have the right moral state first, or you cannot have the art." Tolstoy, recognizing that art was a means of transmitting the artist's feelings to others, held that these feelings must be such that the great mass of the people could understand them, and must promote the love of God and of man.

Today, freedom of the artist to say what he likes and how he likes, is generally accepted. Beyond observing certain restraints on blasphemy and indecency, he is not required, except in totalitarian states and by totalitarian institutions, to further any particular code of morals. The question at issue, therefore, narrows itself down to whether in fact what the modern artist chooses to provide influences morals; and the answer of the modern artist is, "Yes."

To understand this, means returning to the German philosophers. With their aid, the older conception of a necessary connection of art with morals had largely disappeared. Equally with their aid, mainly through the agency of Schopenhauer, the idea of a new kind of link emerged. Schopenhauer took the view of his time that subject in art was unimportant; but following the trend of German philosophical opinion since Kant, held that reality lay not in the phenomenal world, but in the mind. The real world was not that of appearances, but of the ideas that lay behind them; and it was with these that the artist should be concerned. Thus, the value of a work of art depended on the artist's capacity to penetrate beyond appearances. This certainly establishes no connection of art with morals; but it disposes of the idea that the artist's concern is with appearance, and establishes a purpose for art beyond that of giving pleasure.

A comparable development took place in the thinking of architects. Henry van de Velde, the Belgian, enunciated the concept of "fitness for function," the basis of which was that a building (and, by implication, other works of art) should express its purpose in its design. Thus, appearance in architecture should not primarily aim to please, but is to be determined by its structure; a view akin to Schopenhauer's that the artist should express reality behind appearance. At the same time, "fitness for function" also struck a definitely moral note; that good architecture forbade deceit. These ideas have profoundly influenced much modern art. They ruled, for example, in much of the work of the Bauhaus, in which Walter Gropius was the dominating figure; and persist still among some former members of the group and their followers. Broadly, their creed seems to be that, for architecture to be good, it must be honest in the sense of self-revealing. Whether what is revealed is either agreeable to look at, or serves its purpose well, is another matter.

Painters and sculptors on the whole have been more explicit as to their aims than architects. Theirs, after all, are among the "imitative arts" of Plato; and with the virtual bankruptcy of Impressionism and its stress on reproducing appearance, something had to be put in its place. Whether any of them ever read Schopenhauer is doubtful; but his ideas were in the air, and artists felt their impact. Gauguin and Van Gogh, for example, both sought to go behind visual appearance, and to make forms and colors symbols of something else. In their case, this something else was not an underlying reality that could be apprehended visually, but ideas concerning the nature of man and his relation to the universe. It is significant that Gauguin could entitle one of his most important paintings *Whence do we come?; What are we?; Whither are we going?;* and that under Gauguin's influence a group of artists should have emerged calling themselves *Symbolists.* Van Gogh was less specific than Gauguin in the metaphysic he sought to express; rather he was the religious mystic who had seen the glory of God and tried to symbolize the vision on canvas.

In line of descent from these two are all those artists who may be grouped together as Expressionists. Such are Rouault, the religious mystic and attacker of social abuses; the Italian futurists, seeking to give pictorial form to a gospel of force in a mechanized world; Kandinsky, the non-representational painter, with color as his main means of expression; Chagall, the painter of fairy tale fantasy; and the Surrealists, some drawing their material from a dream world, some from the workings of the unconscious. The diversity among these and other modern painters is extraordinary; but nevertheless, they have one thing in common—the aim to externalize in form and color the inner character of sentient and non-sentient beings in such a way as to reveal the metaphysical unity among them which lies behind the disunity of appearance. Sometimes the artist is not content with this, and aims directly at affecting conduct; as when Kandinsky held that art should so strengthen the souls of men as to bring about a regeneration of society, or when Rouault reveals the horrors of prostitution or the corruption of justice.

Turn now to another facet of modern art, that which has found inspiration in Cézanne. Cézanne, like Gauguin and Van Gogh, rejected representation of appearance as an artist's job. An inarticulate man, his work and some oracular utterances suggest that he was seeking to put appearance in terms of certain archetypal forms, and to reveal some kind of basic and continuous relation among forms, through integration of design in his paintings. There is no evidence that Cézanne knew anything about modern scientific thought; but his approach to painting suggests some conception of the unity of matter, analogous to the physical theories of today.

From Cézanne descend the Cubists. Like the Expressionists, they felt the influence of Schopenhauer, and rejected appearance to search for reality behind it; but, unlike the Expressionists, they take example from Cézanne, and try to use form as a direct expression of reality, and not as a symbol of a metaphysic. Also, probably under the influence of Pragmatist thinking, they brought into art the concept of reality being dynamic, holding that the idea which is reality changes with period and place; and therefore with period and place the expression in terms of form of that idea must itself change. This approach helps to explain why the Cubists are never purely nonrepresentational; but starting from a definite object, by analysis of its structure and combination of its various aspects into a unified design, seek to present something more fundamental than appearance.

From the Cubists derive the whole group of what may be called geometrical constructionists, such as Mondriaan, Gabo, Pevsner, and Arp. Their work marks a change in the character of the movement. Some of the earlier Cubists, notably Gleizes, Metzinger, and Léger, have held firm to the purely formal conception of their art, and made it depend solely on the direct impact of forms and then relations. Picasso, however, has come to use form as a symbol of political and social ideas, a famous example being his *Guernica*. Here, he has set an example to the geometrical constructionists. With them, the representational elements of Cubism have been discarded; but the direct social value of their art is stressed. Mondriaan and Gabo both seek to influence men toward living more harmoniously together, by the examples of harmony and equilibrium set before them. Gabo, in particular, argues that society has to adjust itself to new scientific concepts of the universe, and to the development of mechanization, and that new forms are needed in the arts, to express the ideas and emotions which dominate the world. It is the artist's business to organize these forms, and so make his work an expression of human aspirations, and a pattern for construction of a new type of civilization.

The claim, here made unmistakably, that art freely conceived and freely practised, itself conduces to morality, is even more specifically affirmed by the apologists for modern art. One of the earliest among them declared that "there are no qualities of greater moral value than artistic qualities, since there is no greater means to good than art"; while in the very recent past, another holds that "the unity of general form with a variety in its elements" leads to "a binding together of our responses into a unified whole, providing us with a model for the organization of our emotional life and the problems of daily existence."

It seems clear from the foregoing that modern art in no sense disregards morals. But in the light of modern philosophy and modern psychological research, the conception of its relation to them differs from that current in the past. Art is thought of as having a power of its own, as a means of cognition without the intervention of intellect, and so being a source of knowledge and inspiration. Thus, to have its activity tied to and limited by a code of morals, is to deny the fundamental character of art. A glance at history bears this out. Despite variations in taste and fashion, it is remarkable how stable are standards of what is good and bad in art, both in space and in time. Today, the art of prehistoric man, of the African Negro, of the Chinese and Japanese, of the Mayan and Aztec, all created in civilizations remote from our own and very different from each other, are nevertheless admired and valued. In contrast, moral values vary widely, and change rapidly with both place and time. So to judge an art by the moral code of the society in which it was produced, is to judge stability by instability.

This, however, is not to say that the artist should leave out of account the morals of the society in which he works. He could not if he would, for these form part of the whole complex which affects his emotions and ideas. Moreover, he may find in the moral problems of his day, stimulus and material for creative activity. But this is far from saying that the artist should consciously set out to teach a moral code, or to solve moral problems. If he feels that to do so is necessary for his art, well and good; but of this he alone can be the judge.

XII

NEW ART AND OLD MORALS—ANOTHER VIEW

BY

JOHN FERREN

If angels fear to tread in certain places, and it is said that they do, one of these places is surely where the relation between art and morals is being argued. As an artist, I have the same trepidation. To this degree I can understand the angels, and fear to be a fool. But to discuss the question at all I will have to exert a little human violence, hack at some Gordian knots and risk some fringed edges lying on the ground.

I believe that the artist today, and always, performs a moral function in society. Actually, today, he performs two moral functions. One is by his example; that is, by following the spirit at the sacrifice of money, prestige, and the comforts thereof. The other emanates from the work itself which, by analogy, is a reflection of moral truth. The question in hand, therefore, is that of the *quality* of the morals as practised in "new art" and their relation to "old morals."

In the example he sets, along with the pure scientist, the artist is in the last untainted outpost of human freedom. Wedded to poverty and solitude, he nevertheless exists. A fact which, while ridiculous to the average citizen, is still grudgingly admired: for the artist does, in following his personal bent, what others cannot or dare not do in present day society.

Concerning the moral truth inherent in the authentic work of art, it is a hidden one, to be found beneath the work's subject matter, sensuality or derived manners. It is always there through the centuries and it was put there by the maker, not the buyer. It is revealed only to the authentic lover of art. (As God is known through Love, so, surely,

133

is art.) There are so few of these today beyond the artists themselves, that discussion immediately oversteps the boundaries of common knowledge.

Trying to define morals for myself, I see them only secondarily as legal or ecclesiastically acquired impositions of conduct and primarily as the correct responses to the varied stimuli which living in this world entails. Correct because they insure and protect the individual's well-being in his society. The artist is, by his openness to and direct involvement with the stimuli of existence, in a position where he cannot take by rote his actions or reactions. He is driven by creative necessity to see without inherited prejudice or invoked authority the source of morals and art which are himself, nature, and God. In this light, his institutional orthodoxy is questionable, if existent. Divorced from the patronage of the church and then from that of society he is, indeed, on a far limb. But like those tropical trees which throw branches which become roots, his experience is crucial and, although of possibly limited application, it may have some "root" value.

I propose that we refuse, for the moment, the dichotomy existing between morality and art; between the "doing," as the gesture which men agree to live by, and the "making" which goes into the work of art, and investigate the "doing" of the "making" of the contemporary artist. We might find, or at least approach, the "meaning" of "new" art and, by analogy, see how it jibes with "old," or, for that matter, "new" morals.

In the act of making of the contemporary artist, what are his attitudes, conscious or unconscious, when he takes his stance before his easel?

1. He is an individual, a person, in pursuit of, if not in contact with, the suprapersonal. He is beholden only to his own truth, the truth of his craft and the truth of his vision. His painting is, therefore, personal gesture which should not be confused with personality gesture. He believes, as it is necessary for him to believe, that to be authentically personal is to be universal. His state is "that of Israel under the judges, every man doth that which is right in his own eyes." Admittedly, this is a dangerous and easily abused position. But one can say of the artist today as Carlyle said of Rousseau, "he was almost

mad but he had the irradicable feeling that this life of ours is *true*—
not a skepticism, theorem, or persiflage but a fact—an Awful Reality."
The artist's present position is that before this "Awful Reality" he can
supersede it only by complete personal honesty. Every element in his
work is first immersed in the acid of the question, "Is it true?"

2. He thus tries to arrive at the essentials of his craft. A horizontal
line does not necessarily denote the horizon, it denotes calm. Blue is
not only the color of the Virgin's dress or a flower or a symbol of
purity, it is first a color which denotes calm and contraction. Prolonged
exposure to it will lower the blood pressure. Red does the opposite
and so on through all the elements. The forms, colors, planes, and
spaces of the artist's craft have basic psychological and physiological
realities beneath and beyond their use for descriptive purposes. This
push through to essentials has entailed cutting through the academic
cant and the dead brush of the unfelt; which leads us to—

3. He wars on the unfelt not only in his craft but in his visual experience of the world and mental experience of ideas. He wars against
the acceptance of outworn convention, intellectual elaboration, the
acceptance of appearance without personal involvement, the shunting
away of fresh but disrupting experience; but—

4. Holding to the felt he knows that it must be dominated and led
into a fresh structure, a sum, a totality. Fresh experience in a fresh
form. From the personal to the absolute, to perhaps a work of art.

By religious analogy the artist's style is Ritual and his success Revelation. Through the outward form he is after the inner reality. Is not
this also a definition of manners and are not manners the "making"
of the idea of morals?

"New" art is clearly after the reality behind appearances. Call it
what you will, but inevitably the word, "spiritual," must be used, no
matter how shopworn it may be. Morals are the rules of conduct
which respect and reveal the spiritual or highest conceptual source of
man. "New" morals would be those that express him in his present
context. "Old" morals would be those which have become cliché,
"unfelt," and superannuated: in other words, rules of conduct which
are not appropriate to our present experience. The opposition between "new art and old morality" is obvious. New expression de-

mands new response. Response is conditioned by morality. Morals which prohibit the response of the full man as he actually is today divorce him from art, as well as himself. In this time, art is investigating realms of feeling and perception that were closed to our immediate predecessors. It has done this, as science has, by resort to the *tabula rasa,* a putting in question of all the acquired procedures, methods, and certainties. This can have unexpected results, to say the least. The bumping against conventional or "old" morals has been among the first results and has also been to many, including, I would imagine, the atom scientists, a sobering one. In this sense, the dialogue between art and morals is a constant experience with the contemporary artist. He cannot, as can the ordinary citizen, ignore it politely or conventionally because the purity of his reaction to the stimuli of existence is the *sine qua non* of the truth or creativeness of his work. This linking of truth and creativeness is the key to the artist's thinking. He "knows" that when he creates he is true, and he knows that when he is "true" to his responses and approaches to his work he is on the road to creation. Thus the old dialogue forms part of the daily life of the modern artist. It is at the core of his existential situation.

The rightness of an authentic work of art is in the perfect ordonnance of its parts: the moving balance of stress, shape, space, and color that releases the rhythm which touches the spirit. This it is that, by *analogy,* parallels the structure of morals; as morality is the balance in action of the personal, social, and religious desires that exist in communal life. These are often opposing forces and their harmonizing is intended not only to restrain violence but to reveal the "divine" in man, if you are religious, or the "superior," if you are not. Deceit, subterfuge, expediency, or falseness of any sort as surely destroys the work of art as it does morality. In reality, art is more strict. The individual can live and even thrive in sin but the work of art can live only in virtue. The morality of the artist is in his "practising virtue" before his art. The morality of his work is simply in the degree to which it is art. To the spectator, art is the road to experiencing living order in the work itself. Its moral good is precisely in this experiencing. Morals are the social rules to express the living order in the order of living. Any quarrel between the two is through some sub-version of their parts. Somewhere a refusal is made to see that they are only analogous to each other. Then comes an attempt of one to dictate to the other. Historically, all such confusions have been disastrous. The "moral" societies, such as the eighteenth century Enlightenment and the Victorian, lost for themselves, as well as for us, the deeper resonance of art by its subjugation to a pedestrian, politically expedient idealism. The "immoral" societies, such as the High Renaissance in Italy, carried a guilt deriving from their misuse of art that could make Botticelli sensitive to Savonarola's reprimand and burn his pictures. I leave comment on our present period to the reader, but from these confusions, current today, we have the cold blooded, unmoved spectator who sees the surface only and promptly deduces a morality or, more usually, a lack of it. From here flows the mistaken strictures, critical ideals, empty platitudes, and invocations of "old" morals that have clouded the reality of art and from which art has so strongly reacted for the past hundred years. And from here also comes the artist, critic, or politician, who thinks that the power of beauty is not enough and would direct the moral actions of the spectator into apelike imitation of a "moral" subject.

The most creative epochs did not confuse the "Beautiful and the Good," but then again, neither did they disentangle them. Under intense esthetic emotion the recalcitrant pair can be fused and melted into one as did Keats in contemplating his Grecian Urn. I think that the "new" artist, in what is actually a very moral attitude toward his work, is tending toward this integration. But this is a creative attitude and experience which is particular to the lover and maker of art. Of two things a unity is achieved and not subservience of one to the other.

The phrase, "new art and old morals," suggests a jousting for position. Here the artist can state only that "morals" are not in the subject of a work of art and never have been. They are at the core of the art work itself, in its "manufacture" (handmaking)—in the rhythm, balance, stress and strain, and living harmony that create the visual reality of the picture. And this implies, by analogy, that "morals" in society are in the acting without of the inner vision which we have of ourselves as human beings under God. If cant and convention or the "unfelt" pervade this field, there we have "old" morals, and "new" art is against it, will oppose it, and will eternally arouse the wrath of the falsely righteous.

XIII

NEW HORIZONS IN HUMAN RELATIONS

BY

HAROLD D. LASSWELL

It is much easier to talk about my subject today than it would have been a few years ago. The behavior sciences have begun to develop a series of findings much more closely connected with the objectives and interests of persons connected with the humanities than was true before.

If you take the conception of science technically you must regard this as a by-product of the development of the psychological, sociological, economic, and other sciences. It is a by-product in the sense that it was not planned that way. Most of the specialists in this field if interrogated would of course indicate that they are men of goodwill; but within recent years it has been much more important to them to show that they were also men with methods rivaling the physical scientists'.

Consequently, what I am to summarize here are fortunate by-products of this effort to understand human relationships. As I shall indicate, I believe the main significance of what has been happening in the social sciences is this: there has been a development of analysis and of results that emphasize the importance of values other than wealth in the social process and in the lives of people.

The Affection Value

To you this is certainly no overwhelming revelation; and what I am going to say is not intended to be a revelation. What I am saying is that the findings that have emerged from these years of activity by psychologists, sociologists, and others have clarified somewhat the processes by which values in this culture of ours and in some other cultures affect one another.

I will take as my point of departure the report of some studies initiated by engineers which led ultimately to discovering the great importance—not of simple physical factors in production or, indeed, of wealth incentives—but of the significance of affectionate and congenial human relationships. Let me go back to the period of the Taylor System, a very important development in modern industrial society. The people who started off with this kind of human engineering had in mind supplementing the ordinary wage incentives in factories by lightening the load of labor. Part of the purpose of job analysis was to reduce painful work. Thus—and one sometimes forgets this aspect of the objectives of those early pioneers—one of the principal aims was to adjust industry to people so the human beings who work could live more satisfactorily. Many workers did, as a matter of fact, escape from forms of toil that were painful, awkward, and disagreeable; and they enjoyed these advantages in addition to whatever improvements were made in take-home pay.

However, this produced a new major problem, to wit, boredom. Often when the industrial engineers had done their work beautifully and had demonstrated again that the shortest distance between two points is a straight line movement, the workers who were left to operate in straight lines found themselves bored. And presently a number of researches began to focus around the fatigue that boredom was producing in industry. In the 1920's, for example, there were a number of investigations of fatigue. In those days "fatigue in industry" was one of the great slogans in the name of which social scientific operations were conducted. What presently occurred was that the investigations which were supposed to be exploring fatigue, boredom, and monotony began to reveal other factors that were quite important. It is in this connection that I refer to the work and the name of the late Elton Mayo.

It was Elton Mayo with his studies of human relations in modern industry who developed some of the most convincing demonstrations of the point that congenial human relationships among the members of work teams are of fundamental importance, not only for maintaining production, but for satisfactory human relationships among the workers in and out of the factory. What was done was to rediscover by elaborate procedures the degree to which people are dependent upon one another for emotional, for affectional support in the conduct of life. And this remarkable rediscovery has had great effects on modern management.

Of course, the rediscovery of the importance of affection has been highlighted by many other investigations besides those to which I have just referred. Possibly the most startling demonstration of the importance of affection to human beings is the study of what happens to infants in the first year of life. Taking certain hospitals and orphanages as a center of investigation, some research workers noticed once more the traditionally high mortality which these infants suffered during the first year. They decided to experiment by keeping the strictly medical regime constant, and by introducing people who would take more of a human interest in the infants, spend time with them, cuddling them, stimulating them. Some very remarkable results came of this. The mortality rate declined sharply. Here again was a striking example of the dependence of human beings at very early stages of growth on an extra outpouring of affection from their environment.

Another striking exemplification of the importance of affection is a by-product of studies of deviational behavior: criminals, delinquents. I cite a recent study made in Detroit. Incorrigible youngsters were chosen for the research. What was done was to comb Detroit for the most obnoxious brats. Brought together in one house this prize collection provided magnificent research material. (I am happy to report that several of the experimenters are still alive.) The result was to disclose once more the profound point that these incorrigibles were incorrigible thanks to the failure of affectional support from the early environment. They were not sufficiently discouraged to die in infancy; on the contrary, they responded with enough vigor and aggressiveness to assault and provoke their environment. These incorrigible juveniles are oriented toward the rest of us with hate, suspicion, destructiveness. Under the apt and shocking title, Dr. Fritz Redl and his associates report on *Children Who Hate*. And this is one of the most striking exemplifications, albeit a negative demonstration, of the power and role of affection.

The Skill Value

I put the emphasis on the affection value; but a great many of these investigations of human relationships have underlined other values as well. I will mention one which can be disposed of rather quickly: the importance of skill to human beings. Once more we had a rediscovery and demonstration of the importance to human development of opportunities for the maturing of latent talents into socially acceptable skills. The importance of this development was exemplified in connection with the factory studies. After the early wave of enthusiasm for the Taylor System passed, new forms of human engineering were developed in which emphasis was put on the creative impulse in industry. This was the title of a famous book which was widely read at the time and served as a slogan for a great many investigations of human affairs. The point was worked out in detail that many people are misfits, and have miserable lives because they have not had an opportunity to discover their hidden capabilities.

It is through modern researches on aptitude that it has become possible to assist more people in their early years to discover latent capacities. I suppose the most striking demonstrations of the importance of opportunity for the acquisition and exercise of skill for human development have been made in the schools. Any number of difficulties with bright children have been shown to stem from the absence of challenge to develop skills (of a socially acceptable kind, I should hasten to add). There is often a sort of malnutrition of skill opportunities. So far as "dull" children are concerned, one of the most striking developments of recent times has been to show that in many cases the dullness was with the environment and not with them. The environment was dull enough to expect them to acquire only those scholastic skills standard to the curriculum. In many cases the dull youngsters have been demonstrated to have very special aptitudes, once the particular opportunities which bring out these latent abilities are made available.

The area of the skill value must certainly be added to affection as a dimension of human relations which has been illuminated by the findings of the behavior disciplines.

The Enlightenment Value

We can add another value to those whose importance has been stressed, a value that is very close to all of us, namely, enlightenment. We are becoming more aware than ever before of the many difficulties that arise in human affairs because of the failure to enlighten people about what is going on, about the trends in the social process of which they are part, including estimates of the future.

Among other ways, failures of enlightenment show themselves in failures to recognize the "cues" enabling people to master frightening new situations. Psychological analysis has shown that it is quite possible to prepare large numbers of people to meet new and horrifying deprivations, if those individuals are enlightened in advance about what is likely to happen. This means spelling out the cues by which they can identify what is coming up. A succinct little book, *Fear in Battle,* was written by John Dollard in the recent war period. The purpose was to outline in the simplest possible terms the ways by which human beings can overcome fear by the development of enlightenment, by discovering in advance the sorts of cues that would emerge. Imagine the difference between civilian populations, one unaware of the probable structure of the future, and of how to anticipate the buzz-bomb, and the other with a clear image of such a danger. Or imagine troops unaware of how to differentiate the noise of one shell from another. The stability introduced by correct anticipatory training has been demonstrated at home and at the front. By receiving proper enlightenment each one prepares himself in advance to recognize a developing threat, and to keep his mind alert and active. The likelihood is enhanced that the individual can maintain his integration in new and threatening situations.

So we are learning again from these studies the extraordinary importance to human beings of having access to a relevant flow of information about the past and critical estimates of the future. The point has been repeatedly demonstrated in less dramatic ways than those I have referred to. It is quite clear on the basis of many investigations that disciplinary problems, not only in the armed forces or among civilians under fire, but in any group whatever, can be considerably reduced when the participants are enlightened about the position they occupy in the flow of events.

It is important never to neglect the enlightenment value, whose role is constantly covered up in our culture by the tendency to justify a great many choices as sensible in terms of dollars and cents. The main point often is that choices are significant in other terms, simply in improving access to enlightenment.

The Rectitude Value

Another value, that is peculiarly close to us in this Institute for Religious and Social Studies, is that of rectitude, the sense of responsibility for molding conduct in such a way as to contribute to significant goals. No one connected with this series needs to be reminded of the fundamental importance of the sense of rectitude to human beings. It is a deplorable fact that in our civilization there has not only been an overly condensed analysis of human motivations, but there has been a failure to recognize the role of more subtle values than wealth and power. This stricture applies with special force to the role of the rectitude value in the social process.

In connection with rectitude I will refer to the results not of experiment but of tragedy. The behavior scientists are far better equipped than before to probe into and to understand the significance of the people who came out of concentration camps not only alive but highly integrated. The comparative studies of "who responded how" to the brutalizing environment of the camps have indicated the enormous importance of the demand for rectitude—of this feeling of the great importance of each bearing his responsibility for the larger enterprise of which he is a part; the conservation, so far as each possibly can, of significant values. The concentration camp results have indicated that individuals with intense convictions, clearly ideological, religious or secular, were among the most successful, not simply as survivors, but as integrated persons who demanded of themselves that they act responsibly at all times.

The Respect Value

I reminded you of the point that a great many investigations of modern behavior were carried out by engineers who were primarily concerned with technical factors in production and distribution. As these studies broadened, they called attention to the dependence on other values of many factors that we talk about as "economic." The factory researches are especially convincing in relation to affection and skill. Quite a different body of scientific inquiry has illuminated the signal importance of another neglected value, namely, respect.

The work of W. Lloyd Warner and his associates in analyzing the class structure of American society and of some other societies is well known. The importance of respect gradations in a community has received great emphasis in these studies. Professor Warner, among other things, called attention to the point that in many old communities six respect classes are recognized by the members of the community. In some newer cities one of these social groups (the "old family" upper class) drops out, and only five are left. In small communities you may get down to where there are only two ("respectable" and "not respectable").

What is the significance of these mutual respect evaluations? Thanks to the field work of many investigators, the extraordinary impact of a low, middle, or high respect position in shaping human demands, expectations, and loyalties of people has been spelled out in great detail. The role of respect is often far more potent than the comparatively small monetary differences involved.

Multiple Values in Psychosomatic Diagnosis

I shall bring this summary to a close by calling attention to the illuminating results that have come from psychosomatic studies, the studies of physical and mental well-being. I suppose that our period of the twentieth century will be remembered, if it is remembered, partly for the popularity of a great many scientific slogans; and one of them is certainly "psychosomatic medicine." It ought to be "sociosomatic" medicine, because most of the investigators are looking into more than the upsets of an individual organic and psychic system. They are registering the difficulties that arise between two or more people in which somebody's "soma" gives way.

These psychosomatic investigations have emphasized to an extraordinary degree the dependence of physical well-being as a value upon the other values with which we have been concerned: affection, skill, enlightenment, rectitude, respect. What is demonstrated over and over again is that people are often suffering from hidden hatreds and hostilities. These have arisen in the course of their human relationships; and the destructive aggression is turned back against the self in the form of heart trouble, ulcers, headaches, and the like. The interpersonal difficulty may have arisen in reference to affection, as when the sufferer is reacting against indifference or the withdrawal of love. The deprivation may be in the sphere of respect, involving exposure to ridicule and contempt. Perhaps the deprivation involves skill, originating in exclusion from an opportunity to discover and to develop latent capacities. Or the difficulty is in reference to enlightenment, and involves the impact of uncertainties and anxieties arising from lack of relevant cues to the understanding of recurring threats. The source of the trouble may be in relation to rectitude. One may be assailed as immoral, respond with feelings of guilt, and eventually with bodily disturbances. Hence exclusion from the enjoyment of any number of values frequently turns out to precipitate psychosomatic (sociosomatic) upsets.

In these pages I have given a few examples of the sort of findings that modern behavior scientists have been making. I have stressed the point that the main significance of these findings, though in a strictly technical sense by-products of scientific query, is to increase our insight into and our means of affecting the course of human life.

CONTRIBUTORS TO "NEW HORIZONS IN CREATIVE THINKING" *

GEORGE BOAS, Ph.D., University of California; Professor of the History of Philosophy, The Johns Hopkins University; Author: *A Primer for Critics, Essays on Primitivism and Related Ideas in the Middle Ages, Wingless Pegasus,* and others.

OSCAR J. CAMPBELL, Ph.D., Litt.D., Harvard University; Professor Emeritus of English and Chairman of the Department, Columbia University; Author: *Shakespeare's Satire, The Living Shakespeare,* and others.

MELVILLE CANE, A.B., LL.B., Columbia University; Author: *Poems: New and Selected, A Wider Arc, Making a Poem,* and others.

W. G. CONSTABLE, M.A., University of Cambridge; Curator of Paintings, Boston Museum of Fine Arts; Member, Board of Directors, Conference on Science, Philosophy and Religion; Author: *John Flaxman, Venetian Paintings,* and others.

HENRY D. COWELL, Adjunct Professor in Music, Columbia University, 1953–1954; President, American Composers Alliance; Author: *New Musical Resources, American Composers, The Nature of Melody.*

JOHN FERREN, Painter; Instructor of Painting, The Cooper Union; Lecturer in Art, Queens College.

ALBERT HOFSTADTER, Ph.D., Columbia University; Professor of Philosophy, Columbia University.

WALTER KERR, M.A., Northwestern University; Drama Critic, *The New York Herald Tribune;* Author: (Plays) *Sing Out, Sweet Land, Touch and Go,* and others.

HAROLD D. LASSWELL, Ph.D., The University of Chicago; Professor of Law and Political Science, Yale University; Member, Board of Directors, Conference on Science, Philosophy and Religion; Author: *Power and Personality, National Security and Individual Freedom, World Revolution of Our Time,* and others.

R. M. MACIVER, D. Phil., Edinburgh University, D. Litt., Columbia University, Harvard University; Lieber Professor Emeritus of Political

* As of October, 1953.

147

Philosophy and Sociology, Columbia University; Member, Board of Directors, Conference on Science, Philosophy and Religion; Member, Executive Committee, The Institute for Religious and Social Studies; Author: *Community—A Sociological Study, The Modern State, Society —Its Structure and Changes, Leviathan and the People, Social Causation, Democracy and the Economic Challenge, The Web of Government, The More Perfect Union,* and others; Editor: *Group Relations and Group Antagonisms, Civilization and Group Relationships, Unity and Difference in American Life, Discrimination and National Welfare, Great Expressions of Human Rights, Conflict of Loyalties, Moments of Personal Discovery, The Hour of Insight;* Co-Editor: Symposia of the Conference on Science, Philosophy and Religion.

WILLIAM G. ROGERS, A.B., Amherst College; Book Editor, Associated Press; Author: *Fluent French for Beginners, Life Goes On, When This You See Remember Me: Gertrude Stein In Person.*

ROBERT SAUDEK, A.B., Harvard University; Director, TV-Radio Workshop, The Ford Foundation.

BEN SHAHN, Painter; Author: *Paragraphs on Art,* and others.

HARLOW SHAPLEY, Ph.D., Princeton University, etc.; Harvard College Observatory; Member, Board of Directors, Conference on Science, Philosophy and Religion.

INDEX

Abel, Walter, 97-98
Abnormality, in literature, 54, 74, 75
Absolutism, 20
Adolescence, novels of, 54
Affection, in human relations, 139-142
After Many a Summer Dies the Swan, 84
Afternoon of a Faun, The, 40
Age of Innocence, The, 52
Algren, Nelson, 51
All the King's Men, 43
Altruism among insects, 4
American Tragedy, An, 52, 53
Anarchy, 22
Anderson, Maxwell, 108
Anderson, Sherwood, 52, 53
Animals:
　artifacts and ceremonies of, 2
　dominance of man over, 3
Antigone, 12
Ants, 4
Applied science, 17-18
Aquinas, Thomas, 109-110
Archilochus, 107
Architects, "fitness for function" thinking of, 128
Aristotle and the artist, 125
Arnold, Matthew, 29
Arnow, Harriet, 54
Arrowsmith, 52
Art and the arts:
　categories of, 97-98
　as communication, 106
　conscious control in, 15
　and contemporary life, 25-45
　creative and increative, 137
　decadence in, omens of, 68
　diversity in, 23
　estheticism in, 44
　European movements, 96, 98
　evocation through, 35, 38, 41

Art and the arts: (*cont.*)
　exploratory period, 96-97
　expressionists, 75-76, 129
　functions performed by, 25-26
　galleries, 99
　German philosophers and, 128
　government regulation of, 123
　humanist current in, 98
　imagination and, 27-29, 38-41
　of imitation, Plato and, 124
　and industry, 127
　inner tension of, 43
　innovation in, 18
　limitations of, 42
　living as, 15-24
　"The Maze," 97
　as medium, 39-41, 42
　"The Monster," 97-98
　moral influence of, 124
　museum activities, 98
　new, and old morals, 123-138 (*see also* Moral aim in art*)
　non-conformity in, 95
　"The Order," 98
　patronage of, 99, 126
　Phoenixlike character of, 101
　as play, 108-110
　poetry, source of wisdom, 29-31
　psychoanalysis and, 96
　realization and, 31-45
　recession of moral aim in, 126
　Renaissance, 125, 137
　schools and movements, 19
　spiritual response and, 37-38, 39
　subjective dimensions of consciousness, 36-37
　Surrealists, 76, 129
　Symbolists, 129
Art for art's sake, 28, 127
Artificial practises, 21

149